Looking through the Lens of...

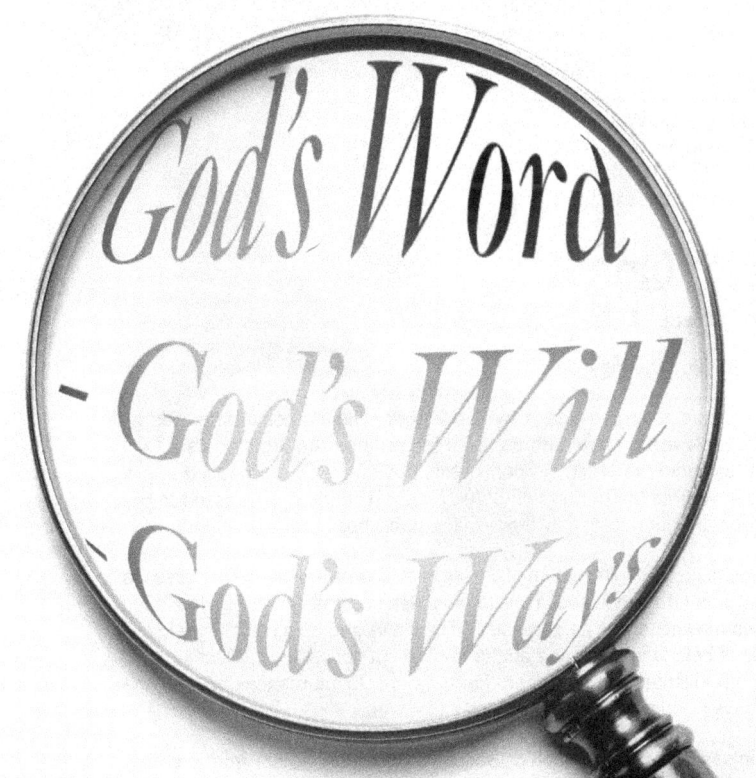

- God's Word
- God's Will
- God's Ways

Dianne Horne

XULON ELITE

Xulon Press Elite
2301 Lucien Way #415
Maitland, FL 32751
407.339.4217
www.xulonpress.com

Xulon Elite

© 2023 by Dianne Horne

All rights reserved solely by the author. The author guarantees all contents are original and do not infringe upon the legal rights of any other person or work. No part of this book may be reproduced in any form without the permission of the author. The views expressed in this book are not necessarily those of the publisher.

Due to the changing nature of the Internet, if there are any web addresses, links, or URLs included in this manuscript, these may have been altered and may no longer be accessible. The views and opinions shared in this book belong solely to the author and do not necessarily reflect those of the publisher. The publisher, therefore, disclaims responsibility for the views or opinions expressed within the work.

Unless otherwise indicated, Scripture quotations taken from the Holy Bible, New International Version (NIV). Copyright © 1973, 1978, 1984, 2011 by Biblica, Inc.™. Used by permission. All rights reserved.

Scripture quotations taken from the Holy Bible, New Living Translation (NLT). Copyright ©1996, 2004, 2007 by Tyndale House Foundation. Used by permission of Tyndale House Publishers, Inc.

Paperback ISBN-13: 978-1-66288-113-8
Ebook ISBN-13: 978-1-66288-114-5

Table of Contents

Preface ix
Dedication xi
Can You Believe it? It Began with Cookie Dough! 1
You Wouldn't Want to Use My Apple Pie ...
Would You Lord? 5
House for Sale ... and Everything in It! 8
Just Standing There on the Corner 14
The Ball That Went Over the Fence 20
Guess Who's Coming for Dinner? 25
Rock Arrangement 29
What's Going on in Your Neighborhood? 34
Downtown Friendships – Part 1 39
Downtown Friendships – Part 2 45
So That's Your Favorite Color! 51
Guess Who Is Receiving Mail? 55
A 7 AM Latte Delivery 59
Who Takes in Your Garbage Can? 63
We Met in the Parking Lot 68
Portable Commode: "Johnny-On-The-Spot" 71
Just Checking in to Say Hello 74
The Gift of Refreshment 80
Fireplace Dining at a Very Tiny Table! 83
How Are You ... Really? 88

Come and See Me ... Anytime.	91
Help for a Friend ... for Such a Time as This	96
A 3 x 5 Birthday Card	101
Honesty at the Bank	104
Can You Teach Me to Sew?	107
Always Be Yourself – No One is More Qualified: Even if you are in Rollers.	112
Making a Difference for One!	116
Learning to Push & Pull	123
Delights in the Double Semi	128
Overnight on a Boat.	132
A Word of Encouragement	136
On the Loose at Night.	141
Royalty in Rollers.	145
A Wealthy Relationship	149
An Honoring Gesture	155
Compassion – Up Close & Personal.	158
Remembering the Losses of Others – Part 1	162
Remembering the Losses of Others – Part 2	167
Making a Difference When you Least Expect It.	171
The Gift of Our Words: The Expression of Our Heart!	175
Uncluttering Our Hearts: Finding Balance in our Values, Priorities & Activities	182
Not in My Lifetime!.	189
What's That I See in Your Pantry?	198
The Attentiveness of God	201

Just One Amongst the Crowd	210
New Soil for a New Season	213
Living a Compelling Life	216
What is Your Calling? What is Your Passion?	220
In Honor of Your Birthday	224
Gardening in my Heels	227
A Lingering Fragrance	229
Tea For Two	233
Roses in the Bushes	237
A Pharmacy Letter: A Prescription of Encouragement	239
When God Says No	243
An Adoption Story – Part 1	251
An Adoption Story – Part 2	258
Flying First Class	265
May I Wash Your Feet?	271
Ordinary	277

Preface

Are you living at a spiritual airport – contentedly watching people coming and going to and from amazing destinations? Though you want to go, you are too fearful of boarding a plane.

Often God's plans require you to take that first step – to relinquish your comfort and begin an incredible journey with Him.

Airport living does not really provide inner joy, peace and purpose. While a world of discovery awaits us, we settle for meaningless *positive experiences*!

Such superficial and momentary events are like reading travel brochures, but never taking the trip.

God arranges "Divine opportunities" to go beyond our comfort zone daily, though we have to ask Him to lead us. Once our bags are packed, we begin our journey of encountering others through meeting their needs.

Loving others requires us to leave the "comfort of the airport," and journey forth in confidence and reliance upon our Heavenly Father.

In this book, I have written about a few of my life-experiences, and the joy I have received through loving others. I have left the airport ... and never returning!

Dedication

These stories originated in the heart of God for my life. As I look back, I can clearly see His handiwork orchestrating each page, and each event of my life. Even before I gave my life to Jesus Christ, He was working within me in my journey, and moving me toward Himself.

This book is dedicated to Jesus Christ, the real and amazing "Author" of these stories. My prayer is that anyone who reads them will be motivated to allow God to edit "their moment-by-moment, and day-by-day journey in life" for His glory.

Yes, we are called to live in such a relationship with Jesus Christ that our lives produce a yearning for Him in the lives of others, not admiration or commendation for ourselves.

Thank you to all the mentors and friends who have enriched my life through their loving example of how to live "transparently." Also, a personal "thank you" for encouraging me to write this book.

Each of your lives, uniquely displayed, have blessed my walk with the Lord through your consistent expressions of the grace, gentleness, and patience of God.

Can You Believe it? It Began with Cookie Dough!

A lot has happened during my lifetime. One event that occurred over 40 years ago was a Divine encounter with God … in my kitchen. God had it all planned, but He needed to get my attention first.

My encounter with God, or I should I say, His encounter with me, occurred around 10 pm … at my kitchen sink. Our small home was again full of international visitors. By this time of the evening, they and my husband had turned in for the night.

While trying to clean up a sink full of bowls and dishes, and with my hands filled with cookie dough, I was having a first class "pity party." I thought back to a number of exciting ventures I'd had before I was married. Now, in contrast, this evening I was here alone, tired, and wondering how my efforts in the kitchen would, or could ever reach a world with the love of God.

I can still remember it as though it happened last night. As my tears began to flow, and being careful to keep them from becoming part of the cookie mixture, I looked out my kitchen window into the darkness, and this thought came into my mind:

WHAT IS IN YOUR HAND?

I somehow knew right away that God was speaking softly to my heart. I remember saying through my tears, "COOKIE DOUGH, LORD–that's what's in my hands–that's all I have to offer you."

He responded very clearly, "I CAN USE COOKIE DOUGH OR WHATEVER IS IN YOUR HANDS ... WATCH WHAT HAPPENS IF YOU JUST GIVE IT TO ME!"

Instantly I had peace. I finished baking the cookies and went off to bed. The next day I didn't say anything to anyone, but I was reminded of the question that the Lord asked at my sink.

I began thinking that this was the same question God asked Moses when he was holding a staff in his hand. Of course, God knew what Moses had, but He wanted Moses to understand it. God knew that all I had in mine was cookie dough.

Later that morning God and I had a ping-pong exchange that started with: "Take half of the cookies you made to your next-door neighbor!" My response: "But I don't know them and I should at least be acquainted with them or at least be introduced in order to do that." "You will, after you take them the cookies." End of dialogue.

After sorting out two dozen cookies and wrapping them in foil, I put one leg ahead of the other and started the long walk next door to my Canadian neighbor, and with my heart racing, I knocked on the door.

I thought neighbors were to reach out to the *new neighbors*, but I found out that God doesn't always work like that. His ways are so radically different. When the door opened, I introduced myself as the new neighbor next door.

I told my neighbor I just wanted to share some cookies I had baked last night, and I nervously handed over the package. She took it, offered a soft-spoken "Thanks," and closed the door.

Every week or so, I'd take over cookies, muffins, or half a cake. This went on for months. Each time I went over, little by little, the woman became friendlier. After a few months, she invited me in for coffee, and in the following months it progressed to dinners, barbeques and then wall papering together.

About ten months later, when my husband was out of the country, to my complete surprise, they asked me to attend a Christian outreach event with them that had been widely advertised. I went. It was a Canadian crusade by the evangelist Terry Winter. At the end of the evening those present were asked that if they realized their need of God's forgiveness and need for His presence in their lives to come forward.

To my utter surprise, they both got up and headed toward the front of the arena. After this evangelist prayed with the mass of people, they returned to where I was seated.

As we were walking out of the coliseum to the parking lot, the neighbor man asked me, "Do you want to know what it was that made us want to attend this event and to give our lives to Christ tonight?"

"Yes" was my response. I had been praying diligently every Thursday for them, but I just couldn't imagine why all of a sudden they were interested in God. My neighbor replied, "It was THE COOKIES. You just kept on loving us through desserts and we'd never experienced someone reaching out like that to us—strangers."

I know without any shadow of doubt our prayers DO MAKE a difference and they open diverse opportunities for God's purpose and plans to unfold.

I never realized before this that when God speaks to our heart it's always profound. The night at the kitchen sink, when He quietly asked me in my heart, "what's in your hand?" I realized later that:

- He knew what was in my hands—cookie dough and
- He wanted "me" to see that whatever was in "my" hands, whatever it was, He could use

Thus, regardless of where I was, He could use whatever it was to CREATE A CONTEXT in which another person could be open toward Him.

God's assignments for my husband and me have been strategically arranged in many varied locations. Little did I realize that those few quiet thoughts from Him that night at the kitchen sink, would change my attitude and give me a real compass for MY LIFE'S MISSION.

I can't reach everyone, but I can go to the "next doors" in whatever neighborhood God places us, or touch those He brings in front of me: whether in a kitchen, an office, board room, or a hospital. God is so practical and involved in our "every day of life!" It's not so much what we say to people, but how we choose to treat them. That is what will affect how they feel.

You Wouldn't Want to Use My Apple Pie ... Would You Lord?

Don't you just love it when the Lord seems to ask something of you that's "right up your alley, "and taste buds?" Don't you just *love* the assignments that are complimentary to your emotional digestive track.

Of course, your responses to God's requests are:

+ Yes, absolutely. I'll get right on that
+ I enjoy that person, and yes, I'd be happy to surrender my time on her behalf
+ No problem. I have time and energy to mow their yard
+ I'd love to have that person over for tea, she's easy to talk with and a real pleasure to have around

Well? We probably wish that were the case, but sadly, often it isn't.

This story is not going to be a long one, but I can still feel the sting of obedience when the Lord asked me to share something with someone that wasn't particularly fun to be around.

From the time this couple (our new neighbor) moved into the neighborhood, they just seemed so critical and hard to get along with. I don't think they realized it, but that's how they came across.

We went out of our way to be friendly! They had asked me to do something for them in their home. I thought I could help, so I agreed.

You know God is working on you to build a servants' heart when people treat you like a servant! That's just a bonus statement, but it's true.

I had completed the task they had asked me to help with, and while at their door, I paused before exiting and asked, "Would there be anything else you'd like?"

It was meant to be a joke ... and we all chuckled. He responded with the comment: "Well, an apple pie would be nice."

I laughed all the way off their porch and out to the sidewalk. The man (I discovered later) had a dry sense of humor.

Later I came to appreciate and love them both later on in our relationship. But the current demeanor of our relationship at that time was not warm and cozy....at least from my viewpoint.

We lived next door, so I didn't have far to travel. In my 60 seconds of travel back to my home, the Lord brought to my attention that I had a small apple pie in my freezer.

There are times we wish that God would drop large road signs from heaven with clear directions on our path. But, in a clear, gentle way God spoke to my heart. "I'd like you to take that apple pie that I know is in your freezer and bring it to the couple next door."

My heart was pulsating so much that you'd have almost seen my blouse moving to the beat of my capillaries.

I wish I could say that I was delighted to do that, but I kinda' prefaced this story about being honest. In fact, I wasn't at all "on board" with His current request and assignment!

However, God doesn't ask us if we're in agreement with His wishes, but He does want to enlist us to love others; even the ones who are difficult to love.

I knew if I didn't do what He wanted right away, I might not do the right thing, if you know what I mean. I got the pie out and headed for the long journey next door. A one-minute travel can seem like miles when you're not in the right frame of mind.

I wasn't exactly what you'd call an enthusiastic traveler, but I did arrive at the assigned destination with some reluctance. I hesitatingly pulled out my index finger and reached for the doorbell button, and pressed it.

Surprisingly, they both came to the door, and the only thing that came out of my mouth was: Here's the apple pie you requested!

Both of their eyes bulged to their full capacity, and they began to laugh uncontrollably. "What's this?"

"Apple pie that you requested." And then I left, laughing all the way home. Upon my arrival, the Lord responded quietly. "Thank you for doing that."

From that moment on, our relationship changed. They became our friends!!

Yes, God uses the "ordinary things of life; and creates the extraordinary from our tiny obedience.

Isn't God wonderfully creative, even if we're not in the right frame of mind!

This couple is still very dear to us!

House for Sale ... and Everything in It!

When I look back on my life, it seems as if I've always been "on the move." I mean that! If you have never had friends who were in the service, let me introduce you to "on-the-move" living.

As a child of an Air Force dad, I was all too aware of our family's almost constant relocation. There seems to be some hidden delight in the various branches of the military that requires shifting their personnel about every two years.

Consider the implications of all this moving: just when you get everything in place within your home, make some good friends, know where most of the items are in your local grocery store, your physician actually recognizes you from your last appointment, and you have met several of your neighbors, IT'S TIME TO MOVE.

I'm chuckling as I write this and you may think I'm exaggerating, but it's so close to the truth, it isn't funny.

Where we currently live (notice I said currently), I had transplanted a large bush in the yard in front of the house. A few weeks later I was outside taking an inventory-style look at my work and saw the newly-planted bush sagging and looked very unhappy.

A neighbor appeared and made an insightful observation, "The bush looks dead!" I laughed out loud and responded that it wasn't dead, it had been transplanted just a couple of weeks earlier and it was *adjusting to its new environment.*

The same happens to people who have recently moved to a new location. They can sometimes look very tired, wilted, and sagging in places.

Yes, we've all heard the phrase "bloom where you're planted." But an ingredient in that phrase doesn't discuss the pain of transition when your physical and emotional roots are torn away from one home location and planted in another.

I apologize in advance to our friends who have tried to keep up with the number of "moving transitions" we have made. Thankfully many have cell phones and we won't have to buy them new address books. But let me say this: We are experienced movers and 'adjustment' is our middle name.

In case you have ever wondered who rents those interstate moving trucks ... well, now you know. Though we don't' follow the stock market, we should have bought stock in Hertz-Penske or U-Haul years ago.

However, due to my husband's work, there was one move we anticipated from Washington State to Southern California. I should add that in all of our moves, we have never had a company or a mission pay for our moving.

One evening, my husband invited me to sit down for a talk. Experience told me this is going to be an important discussion. The topic was our upcoming transition (notice I didn't say 'move') to California.

He was crafting together nice phrases prior to the release of his well-intentioned suggestion. *"Let's sell everything in the house, that way we won't have the expense of moving it."* I'm going to pause right now ... and let that sink in.

We had done this "selling of everything" once before, and I was not on board this time. He honored my response, but asked me to pray about it. My wise husband realized that only God would be able to change my mind on this idea.

Now you may be wondering, what did I decide? Was I okay with selling all the furniture? In a word ... NO!

Time passed and we put the house up for sale. People were coming and going through our home, but there were no offers. One day our realtor phoned to say that someone wanted to come view our home and take a video so that he could show his wife who was located on the other side of the United States.

I agreed, and I thought it was a great idea for his wife's benefit.

The time for viewing our home was set for the following day. I knew the ropes of showing a home: everything neat, counters cleared, vacuum as needed, and all the lamps were in the "on" position with personal photographs removed for visual clarity.

Thus, when the house was this ready, I thought to myself, "Yes, I'd like to live here."

The doorbell rang and I greeted the realtor and her client who was very polite and all geared up with a video camera. Not wanting to be part of the 'house on parade' video, I exited through the back door and made my way around to the front door step and just sat there.

Soon, I was invited back inside my home for the usual pleasantries.

Sensing that the client wanted to talk privately with me, the realtor went to her car. The client and I sat on the front steps. He must have told her that he just wanted to ask me questions about the house and there was no need for the realtor to stay.

Are you sitting down? Perhaps you should. The client remarked that he liked the home and thought his wife would enjoy it as well. He said that he would be paying *CASH*! and since we were both Christians, he asked me to pray about the bottom-line selling price that we would be happy with … and he and his wife would do the same.

I quietly gasped for air on this information, as then he made one more inquiry, "*What are you going to do with all your furniture?*"

That didn't take any thought, "We're going to move it with us." Dahhh!!! His next comment brought my jaw to the cement.

"I'd like to buy everything in the house." What??? What do you mean by everything? He said, "All the furniture, lamps, computer, telephone, even some pictures."

It seemed laughable, but I felt like God wanted us to do this, but I had said "no" to my husband; so the bigger guns were in on this. What would I say now? I could hardly get my tongue around the word "yes." I couldn't believe that it came out of my mouth.

After this verbal agreement, we had some laughs and lighter conversation. He knew that my husband wasn't home at the time, but wanted to talk with him further about our discussion. Believe me, I wanted to talk about it too.

As this prospective buyer was about to say goodbye, I invited him for dinner later in the evening ... when he could speak with us both about his offer, or should I say offers. We agreed on a time, and off he went.

Just before entering his car, I remember vividly him saying to me that he was serious about his cash offer and not to worry.

Isn't this just something the Lord would say to one of His children!!!! He then handed me his business card. My eyes focused on the town ... *NAZARETH, PA*. Yes, the Lord's ways are mysterious, and sometimes hilarious.

Within about thirty minutes, I heard the garage door open and Mr. Husband was about to have the surprise of his life. He usually would ask if anything was new. NEW?!! This time I asked *him* to be seated, and I told him that I had just received a cash offer for the house as well.

Now it was time for his jaw to drop southward. He couldn't believe it. Then I went into tears. The tears were the seal of the deal, he knew this was no joke.

I then told him about our dinner plans, our need to pray about the selling price, and to discuss what furniture we would be willing to sell. Referring to our earlier discussion on whether to sell the furniture ... he couldn't believe I said yes to this perfect stranger.

To be honest, I felt as though God used this man to approach me with the offer.

That afternoon we prayed about the amount we would be happy with. We knew our bottom-line price and yet we wanted to be fair with this man.

I don't even remember putting dinner together that afternoon. From the moment the man stepped in the door that evening, it was as though we had been friends for years. We talked about many things and towards the end of the evening; yes, I mean end of the evening, we finally got around to the price of the house and the furniture.

When we shared the amounts that each of us thought was right, both the buyer and we, had unbelievably arrived at the *"same financial figure."*

Then the topic went to the furniture. We rose from the table to walk around the house and look at the items he wanted. He wanted it ALL! Yes, even the old grill outside. If we had a dog and cat, I am sure they would have been included! We were only going to take our clothes and whatever was in our cupboards.

By now, are you gasping for air? This is a *true story* and my heart is rejoicing again in what God did and how He orchestrated it all. The buyer and his wife were thrilled, and my husband and I were beyond happy.

A month or so later, his family moved from Pennsylvania into our home. Within weeks my husband was out of the country, and knowing about his trip away, they asked me for dinner one evening.

While on the telephone, I inquired as to how they were settling in.

They were in and settled in less than two weeks. We all laughed because they shared that they left the furniture in the exact location as I had placed it, so all they and their children had to do was put their clothes away, and place food and dishes in the cupboards.

They shared that it was the easiest move they'd ever made. Well, I should say so.

When this prearranged evening arrived and I entered my "former dwelling place," I could hardly hold back the tears. Memories we had built in that home were flooding my heart. They even took me around to show me the place, as if I required a tour.

It was a process of releasing what we had enjoyed to another family to continue building memories of their own and to enjoy the provision of the Lord.

Lesson here for me: we really don't own what's in our homes, we are just the caretakers of what the Lord has allowed us to enjoy and use for Him.

Just Standing There on the Corner

Haven't we all used the phrase, I was minding my own business when?

We lived in street level condo in a large, metropolitan city in California for a time. From there we saw all kinds of people from around the world pass by our little patio. Some presumably had homes, but we knew many were homeless.

My body needs to have a walk every day, and this story occurred when we only had one car. So, I would walk our dogs in the local park and meander around the city for a few blocks.

This day, I had stepped from our patio area and toward our mailbox down the block, then onto the park for a casual stroll. After clearing our mail box, I felt a strange feeling come over me— as though I was being watched.

I was on a busy intersection at the time, so I wasn't particularly concerned, but in turning around I saw an older man just standing there and looking around.

He seemed lost and was attempting to get his bearings. It's not my custom to talk to male strangers on the street, but I was compelled to take an interest in him.

I took the plunge and said something like "Hello, are you looking for someone?"

He said no, but that he wasn't sure where he was. I had asked if he was new around this area as I hadn't seen him before. Apparently, that struck a chord in his mind.

Yes, he was very new to the area, and said he lived close by with his son. I found out later, he was just across the street from where he was living when we had this brief encounter.

Though there was a gentleness and sweetness about him that was magnetic, he obviously needed someone to come along side and provide direction to where he was going or where he needed to return.

Since I was on my way to the park, I asked if he would enjoy taking a 20-minute walk with me. He happily agreed and I assured him that I would walk him home as well.

I learned he was 81 years young and he was just a delight.

I introduced him to what I thought was a new area to him, just two blocks from his apartment, but he firmly maintained that he had been to that park before.

Heading home with my two little dogs and new friend, we had to cross the street. There were train tracks, trolley tracks and a traffic light.

It was a very busy and often congested intersection of the city. To my amazement, he began crossing the street at the WRONG time, and against the light at the crosswalk.

It was at this point that I sensed that it was by God's special intent that I had encountered this man. He was lost ... in a number of ways. This situation at the lights confirmed the fact.

I was thrilled that my presence was there to 'find him' – since he was at a loss to know what to do at an intersection.

We finally arrived at the front door of his apartment building. You won't believe it ... but his apartment building was directly opposite to where my husband and I were living.

I discovered that this dear man had trouble with his apartment FOB because he had to swipe it in one area, and then proceed to the door before too much time elapsed so he could enter. This was a struggle for him. This became my first, of many hands-on-instructions.

My heart went out to this man and I knew instinctively that this wouldn't be my last interaction with him. Before he successfully entered his apartment building, he inquired if I'd be out walking in the afternoon.

Well, you can just about guess what happened.

I told him where I would meet him, not knowing if he would remember. But no, he was right on time and at the proper location. We met just outside our little patio gate. I chose to exit our building from a different spot to be safe, as I wasn't sure if he should know where I lived.

Goodness, a walk in the park is getting complicated, but God knew what He was up to in this man's life ... and in mine as well.

I won't embellish this true story, but twice each day we met outside our condo and walked.

Each time we walked, I found myself in "traffic class" with him, showing him over, and over, and over, what to look for on the crossing light and when to cross the street. We even covered the stop, look and listen instructions.

He was a marvelous student, and we'd review the instructions every time we came to any set of traffic lights. He was quite proud of himself in all that he was comprehending in his personalized traffic school.

It wasn't until I arrived home in our little condo that I realized I was invited by the Lord into this man's life to provide much needed practical assistance.

After a few days of walking, I could sense his growing dependence upon me. Inquiring minds need to know things that are helpful. By now, I had his cell phone number and his son's name with whom he lived.

He was generous and open with the information, and I was very grateful.

I wondered about this new situation, as it was certainly obvious to me that I needed to be in contact with his son in the event I was a topic of conversation between he and his son. I felt strongly that his son needed to meet me and be aware of our daily rendezvous at the park and why.

As you hear this, you can begin to see my plight. I wanted to help, but I wanted him, and especially his son, to know that I was happily married, and just a companion walker with and for his dad.

Oh my, I so needed to set the stage so that there would be no complications.

I phoned his son and introduced myself to him. He had already heard a lot about me from his dad. Due to his mental capacity, I just wasn't sure what was conveyed to this man's son.

I explained how I met his dad and what our daily routine was and why. His son was very understanding and accommodating and agreed to meet me for a personal introduction on my patio.

The introduction went well, and he was fully aware and sensitive to where I was coming from. I felt more comfortable now walking with his dad, knowing about the details of his dad's dementia.

To hear from this older man's son, he was delighted to know that someone was walking and instructing his dad on the traffic patterns and about the new places to walk and explore.

Meeting with the son wasn't my only agenda as I needed my husband to know the purpose of my new little friendship. It was like a father-and-daughter walk.

One particular day, in our walk together at the closest park, he shared with me about being separated from his dear wife. She lived with their daughter on the other side of the United States and he was now living with his son.

They both needed care from their families, but it brought a new dimension to their marriage and they needed to be separated for a season.

Slowly my new friend began to trust me and open up about his life. To make a long story short, I had the joy of introducing him to Jesus Christ and why He died for him.

I'll never forget the moment, after sharing the gospel with him through many stories and illustrations, when I asked if he wanted to invite Jesus Christ into his life.

To my surprise and delight he said, "Yes." So right there sitting on a park bench, I led him in a prayer. Ten minutes later, he didn't remember it, but God takes us just as we are (in every way).

He may not have remembered what He said to God, but God remembered his conversation with Him ... and that's all that matters.

We enjoyed many months of walking together, having a sack lunch now and then sitting on park benches with my two little dogs. Then the sad day came when we moved to another State. But the day before we moved, his wife had died.

On our last day together, he shared his sorrow with me. My tender encounters with this man had ended, and needless-to-say, I will never know why God moved me away. God knew best.

After we moved away, I continued to phone him often so he would not be alone in his grief. I wanted him to know that I was walking with him, but just at a distance.

God in his grace and love, and through the dementia, he was able to forget his pain and remember his wife, the love of his life, with fond memories. Not too long ago I phoned him, but he did not remember me. But that's not important ... because I will always remember him.

**GOD LOVES US AND TAKES US JUST AS WE ARE....
WHEREVER WE ARE.**

May we never forget that.

The Ball That Went Over the Fence

It was just another ordinary day, and I escorted our two furry companions, a Pomeranian, Winnie and a Papillon, Chelsie, to the tranquil park behind our home.

The dogs were getting restless – I chuckle remembering that the dogs had their routine down to a science, and were waiting for their walk that morning which was an hour overdue.

I gathered their leashes, and picked up their ball, and off we went. The park is bordered by a widely paved path at its perimeter.

The park had recently been fenced off with a 7' high fence-enclosure in the center part of the park.

Our destination was the far corner of the park which had a paved, fenced in basketball court.

The dogs and I would focus on the court at the end of our walks, because I could turn the dogs loose without worrying about them running off somewhere, and we could freely play ball.

Both Winnie, our blonde Pomeranian, and I adored that part of the park, because I could toss the ball and watch her wear herself out retrieving it.

She has enough stamina to retrieve up to 22 tosses of the bright orange ball

which could be seen from a great distance, and was seldom not in her sight.

One morning, as we rounded the last lap around the park, I noticed that a young Chinese lad was practicing his basketball skills. He was occupying our "get the ball, Winnie" court area.

I know the court doesn't have our name on it; but honestly, since we're there daily, around the same time, others should have recognized our commitment to that play time.

We even slowed our approach, hoping this young man would tire of his solo basketball practice. But no, he remained focused on his drills.

I thought of a creative solution. Since this little Pomeranian needed exercise, and knowing she wouldn't leave her ball, I began to toss the ball.

Winnie would run as fast as her little 3-inch-high legs would allow, and she would retrieve the ball in her mouth, and then roll it towards me so we could continue the "ball" game.

This ball was not just an ordinary ball. It was an indestructible one, and for our little blondie, this was important.

Things were going along quite nicely until I over-extended my pitching arm and projected the ball right over the seven-foot-high fence.

I went over to the area and it didn't take me long to figure out that I was not going to be able to get the ball. The fun and games were over.

I paused, and thought perhaps the boy would see me and our "ball dilemma." But no! He continued on – oblivious to our helpless condition.

There was no way I was going to attempt to hike over that fence myself, and resigned myself to the fact that this ball was history and not coming home with us.

With no other possible solution, I figured we might as well go home. Winnie was not a happy camper – she gave me such a mournful look.

I was just about to leave and head home, when God brought a Scripture to mind. Proverbs 3 verses 5 & 6:

> [5] Trust in the Lord with all your heart and lean not on your own understanding; [6] in all your ways submit to him, and he will make your paths straight.

You may wonder how this verse fits into the–ball–over–the–fence scenario.

So, right then and there, I considered the options of returning home, or praying and asking God to help me get that $8 orange ball back where it belonged.…in my hand.

I was still not physically prepared to hop over the fence, but the fact remained that I had 'asked God to help me.' I think if Winnie was human, she would have barked a loud "amen" at the request.

The thought came to me to walk around the park again. I wasn't thinking of the walls of Jericho at the time, but all I knew was that I had asked for God's help, and another walk around the park **gave Him time to come up with His reply.**

This trip yielded a 6' tree branch. I thought, this is God's answer. Ten minutes later we rounded the bend, and the young man was still practicing on the court.

I approached the fence with my "answer to prayer stick," and poked it through the fence to where the ball was laying. Alas, my reach was still two feet *short*.

Just as I was pulling the stick out of the fenced area, I felt someone approaching us. You'll never believe it. It was the young basketball player. He had noticed us and came over.

It was obvious from the start that he could not speak a word of English, and I couldn't communicate in Mandarin Chinese to him.

But by his facial expression and flaying arms, he told me he would climb over the fence and get the ball.

Before I could take a breath, and with electric speed, he hoisted himself over the fence and retrieved the ball.

Winnie was dancing with excitement and enthusiasm as only a little Pomeranian can do, and I was dancing inside with joy myself, thanking the Lord for His intervention in such a "small matter." What a lesson!

You'd better sit down now for the rest of the story!

The Chinese boy was about sixteen. After passing the ball over to Winnie, he came right over to me.

I was so over-joyed....and my body language must have indicated that I wanted to give him a hug. He approached me with his arms extended and gave me a long hug ... a hug like he'd give his mother.

I hugged him back with enthusiasm as well. Young Chinese boys customarily do not behave in that manner, especially to strangers.

"Lord, how do I say thank you to this young guy in Mandarin?" Moments seemed like hours, then my mind kicked in gear, "*Xie Xie*." I shouted out a Mandarin thank you and his eyes grew big as giant marbles.

I wanted him to know I was so appreciative of his kindness.

The young man went back to the court to continue playing and we took off for home. I only know a few phrases in Mandarin, and was thankful that I could remember "thank you."

All the way home I was thanking God for His kindness and provision at the park through a perfect stranger. God is so kind and so aware of our every step and every dilemma.

LOOKING THROUGH THE LENS OF . . .

I'll never get over how God delights to share our days and "ordinary ways" with us.

Guess Who's Coming for Dinner?

It was the Christmas season and I asked the Lord what type of activities we should be creating to celebrate Him. My husband and I have never resided around family, so we've adopted and invited many a dear one to join us in celebrations over the years.

We gather them from church; our neighborhood, and even those to whom we've recently been introduced.

This particular year we wanted to have friends and soon-to-be-friends over for dinner on Christmas Day. Honestly, I have such a wonderful time preparing for these occasions – almost as much as when the people arrive. I think it's called "enthusiastic anticipation."

I wanted the table to be lovely, and the atmosphere filled with God's joy and love for all those who gathered round. We had pared our invitation list to ensure we had time to interact with each person, and felt that eight people would arrange comfortably around our table. The total was seven!

But about six weeks before Christmas, I sensed the Lord nudging me to invite "just one more." This 'one more' was the elderly father of one of our guests.

God nudged my heart that this man needed to be around people because his wife had passed away a few months earlier, and this was the first Christmas he would be alone.

My heart wasn't settled for this additional person. I had never met the man, and I truly wondered whether he would fit in with the other guests.

Honestly, I realize it was a terrible thought, but I've learned long ago that it's a good thing to think about who you want to gather in your home.

Once we had invited a number of "shy and somewhat introverted people" for dinner, and my husband and I had to carry on almost all of the conversation. So, it's good to invite different personalities so that everyone will feel comfortable and included.

The most pressing hesitation was that I had never met this person, and I was wondering how to sensitively "love" this man who had lost his wife just months before.

I didn't want him to feel uncomfortable or out of place. But, in reality I didn't want *me* to feel uncomfortable either. Obviously, I was the hindrance here, and I felt so ashamed.

Though my heart remained unsettled inviting this man, we had already invited his only daughter to come. It was only appropriate to include her father, especially now when he was finding himself in a new place emotionally.

It was time to make that important telephone call, and … no, a "text" would not do. I phoned our friend and asked if her father was available on Christmas day to come and spend the day with us.

Available???!!!!! Are you kidding? He was all alone. I explained that we would love to include her father if he'd feel comfortable in coming and if he had no prior plans.

I also mentioned that and the dress was casual, and we had a comfy chair close by so he could enjoy an afternoon nap after dinner, just in case.

In less than an hour we found out that he was more than available to join his daughter on their first Christmas together without a wife and mother present.

His only hesitation was that "he didn't know anyone" except his daughter, and I still honestly wondered if he would feel uncomfortable. Our friend, his precious daughter, assured him he would be well loved and well looked after.

Weeks passed and Christmas day arrived. My heart and kitchen were overflowing with excitement – it was glorious. The table had been set the day before and all the goodies to eat were fully prepared.

We eagerly looked forward to the arrival of our guests and a new-found friendship.

Everyone was arriving, and the laughter and hugs began. Then came that special moment when our friend arrived with her beloved dad. Whatever nervousness I had previously, slipped away the instant I saw him.

He was greeted with big smiles and a big hug. "We're so pleased you could come!" He just oozed with enthusiasm and smiles. He made my day before he even sat down at the dinner table.

How could we have had Christmas dinner and NOT invite this dear one. God had special plans for this 93-year *young* and youthful man. Everyone at the table made him feel special. He was the star of the show!

We opened our little "Christmas-crackers;" you know, the ones where there is a little gift inside and those funny, abundantly loud color paper hats.

Yes, we made everyone wear those paper hats that day. It was a kaleidoscope of color! The meal went on for several hours, and we just remained at the table after the meal.

As the hours passed, I quietly mentioned the "comfortable chair" that was available in case he would enjoy a little shut-eye from the laughter and talking. You know, *"resting your eyelash"* time.

Are you kidding!? He would have nothing to do with the chair. He didn't want to miss a thing. After everyone quieted down and tummies were full, one by one people began feeling it was time to return to their homes for some relaxation.

We walked each guest to the door and parted with joy and sadness that everyone was leaving. Our 93-year young guest was the first to leave arm–in–arm with his daughter.

The entire group at the table went to the door to say their farewells to him with hugs and kisses. Honestly, you would have thought he was our guest of honor.

They both thanked us profusely for the wonderful time. Honestly, everyone enjoyed each other, but he was meant to be loved in warm and heartfelt ways that day.

In the months that followed, our friend – this man's daughter – thanked us over and over again. She shared with us that this was an over-the-top Christmas for him.

He felt so at home, loved and comfortable with everyone.

A year later the Lord had moved us to another place over a thousand miles away, and we couldn't have these people over for Christmas dinner.

But the weeks before this new Christmas season, guess who phoned to tell us again that her dad's experience that day was incredible! She too had needed to be with people who loved her that emotionally-empty Christmas day following the loss of her mother.

My heart is wired on inviting people who don't have family around because their hearts need a special touch of love and companionship. This man was a gift to not only my heart, but to everyone's heart that was there.

We all need that regular reminder to invite strangers, and allow their presence to enlarge our hearts and lives. We'll be richer for it; I know mine was.

Rock Arrangement

This experience was a unique opportunity to show God's love and *practical* care.

I'm an outdoor, work-in-the-garden and get-your-hands-dirty type of homemaker. There is something therapeutic about moving about in the dirt, rocks and grass. My fingernails can attest to the fact that they've been active participants in my yard care.

More than once women dressed in those cute little jogging outfits have glanced my way as I was bent over or moaning in the garden. When there's sufficient eye contact with one, I smile and respond with the phrase: "some people belong to the gym, I get my work out here in the yard."

This event took place at a time when we lived in the United States where it was very HOT for about six months of the year. It was difficult to see, let alone connect with neighbors since people would drive home from work or shopping in their air-conditioned cars, and pull directly into their garages and seek shelter in their air-conditioned homes.

I'd be the first to admit we did the same. It was just too hot for work or play in the yard! Even dipping into a pool felt like a warm shower.

Over the cooler months I got to know our neighbors. At a balmy 85 degrees, one particularly cool morning I perched in a lawn chair and enjoyed a latte outside our front entry to relax and enjoy an hour of "doing nothing." Yes, doing "nothing" is a wonderful activity sometimes. (in Italian it is referred to as *dolce far'niente*) [Dolchay Farn' nien tay]

My chair was out far enough to notice some activity a few houses down the street. What caught my eye was our neighbor directing a man where to place the rocks in his yard. This "rock formation" layout was to form a water-bed scene in his front yard.

I knew the neighbor in charge of this project, and even from a distance, I thought it was a clever idea. Before too much time elapsed, I found myself walking over to peruse the situation.

I wasn't there long when it was obvious that my neighbor was not happy with the place and the way the rocks were being placed.

My neighbor had outlined how this continuous rock bed formation should look using larger rocks which he had placed, and this hired man was to place the smaller rocks within that layout so that it would resemble a stream-like brook. My assessment of the situation was pretty accurate as I saw the rolling of the eyes and the deep sighing by my neighbor.

The man whom he hired to help out was just tossing the 6" to 8" rocks into the area at random hoping they would look right after landing.

Neither my neighbor, or his hired worker, nor I, had any experience in "rock arrangement;" but I could see that it was looking messy, and frustration was written all over my neighbor's face. A conversation began to take place in my head.

It was this: "I think each rock should be *'arranged'* in this designated area, not just tossed in with the hope it would work out to resemble a river-bed."

Now normally, I would have minded my own business and walked back home, but my inner frustration was mounting, and so was my neighbor's. I thought to myself, this worker needs help.

He needs to be "shown how" to place the rocks, then perhaps he would catch on.

I gently invited myself into this "rocky project" by asking the owner if I could just help out a little, and see what would happen if we would attempt to "arrange the rocks" with care instead of tossing them in at random. At this point, he certainly had a *more than cooperative spirit to that idea*!

Now I need to insert here, that earlier in the week I had asked the Lord to use me in our neighborhood and create practical "opportunities" to love others, as He loved them. Well, the opportunity became abundantly clear that this was it, and was ever-so-close to home.

The task at hand required you to get on your knees. I found that if I took each rock and placed them like the piece of a puzzle, to both fill and overlap the dirt, it would begin to take shape. After about ten minutes of puzzling the rocks together, it started to look like a stream.

The owner, my neighbor, was thrilled that this array of rocks was beginning to come together in the stream-like fashion he envisioned.

Before long (about two hours later), I had completed over a third of the "rock arrangement" in his front yard. I never looked up to see what the other man was doing, but I think he was given a new assignment. That being: just bring the rocks from the truck and dump them close to where I was kneeling.

The hours went by, and before the end of the morning, the "stream" was halfway completed.

The following morning the worker never showed up at my neighbor's home. You guessed it, I found myself "cheaply employed" by our neighbor. I say cheaply because my earnings came through smiles, not cash.

We both agreed to start the completion of the stream very early the following morning. Now it was just the two of us playing with these rocks.

My neighbor was a tall, slim man, and my build is much closer to the ground. He wisely suggested I needed knee-pads for protection from callouses. Good idea ... I used his. This time I was dressed appropriately for the job, very old clothes, and a ball cap with a pair of "tight-fitting" knee-pads.

Trust me, it wasn't a pretty picture; but who cares, you're playing in the dirt.

Laboring together was fun (did I say fun?). He would scoop out the rocks from the truck, and dump them close by so I could just reach out and grab a rock and continue the sorting and placement.

To be honest, I was really "into my work." Things were progressing quite well and the "creek formation" was clearly coming together.

We were on a roll, as they say, until we were interrupted by neighbors driving by and stopping to ask: "who's the little boy you have working for you?" My neighbor, the task manager of this project, began to laugh.

My focus was on the rocks, but when the pile of what I was forming was empty, I wondered why he had stopped doing his end of the job.

I rose up slowly (and I mean slowly ... as my back was getting sore) and found several pairs of eyes perched in my direction. Accompanying the eyes was laughter.

They were laughing at the fact that they thought I was a boy. My "rock boss" told them who I was and they couldn't believe it.

At this, I was prompt to take off my hat and reveal my true identity. I'm a girl for goodness' sake!

This just brought on more laughter. After my six foot plus boss ceased his chuckling, we resumed the routine of our work. About an hour later, the CREEK BED WAS COMPLETED!!!!

I even lost a few pounds during that task. But I will never forget the fun and sense of joy in helping out my neighbor. And most of all, realizing that this was "God's practical assignment" for me that week to show this man something of God's love and care for him.

So, if you're interested in being a channel for God to use in your neighborhood, may I suggest driving with your eyes fixed straight ahead as you never know who might need "your helping hand ... on God's behalf."

I must add that about a week later my neighbor came over and presented me with a lovely gift ... my own "new knee-pads."

What's Going on in Your Neighborhood?

Your presence, in 'your' neighborhood contributes toward creating a compelling environment in which your neighbors can see Christ in action.

Expressing the love of Jesus Christ to others in practical ways demonstrates our relationship with Him by caring for others.

There are numerous avenues to reach out and touch someone in ways that 'honor them' and show them that 'they're special.' The sky is the limit.

God chooses to *use people ... to connect with others* for Him. In order to be a blessing to another, we need to engage ourselves in the lives of others. This is usually done through our hands, feet, ears, hearts, eyes, mouth and mind.

I've thought ... what can I do? I'm only one. Yes, one plus Almighty God.

What character qualities or attitudes do I need to embrace in order to begin building a "compelling environment" that will draw others to God's love?

Here are a few thoughts on closing the social gap:

First, leave home, but leave your_self_ at home. Take walks with your children or pet. Once outdoors, you will be noticed by people in your neighborhood.

Hibernation can suffocate you, and can even bring on unneeded depression, mild or otherwise.

Second, get out of your comfort zone ... again it's your house. Yes, it's where we feel safe and secure, but it's also where 'nobody on the outside knows your name.'

In retail, the adage is: "If customers can't see it, they can't buy it."

Third, just be a joy to see. I'm not talking about how you dress but how your facial countenance appears. A *smile does increase our face value!*

Try to issue as many smiles to others as you can. It's amazing that many will smile in response to your first attempt at a facial upward curve.

If we walk often enough, we'll begin to see the same people out with their kids, dogs, walkers and friends.

Most of the friendships I've developed have been because I have smiled first, and through that I've made an attempt to be friendly.

Fourth, forget yourself. My husband and I have been NEW to twenty-nine neighborhoods thus far, and trust me, people care more that you have a friendly, caring attitude, and less that you're new.

You may feel strange and awkward at first ... but that's because your focus is on you. May I tenderly repeat: forget yourself.

A little like wearing a team jersey, our identification with the Savior comes naturally. The "you" part – being self-conscious – soon fades into the background as you focus on just being friendly.

No, I'm not talking about dripping over people ... just a gentle hello accompanied by a smile. Watch and see what happens. If you belong to the Savior, just get out there and represent Him.

I remember a woman asking me one time: "How can you be new and just reach out in friendliness to others? Don't you feel self-conscious?" I responded yes, and that's the problem. I have to *get over myself.*

I shared with her that many times I sense God saying to me as I drive around a new environment where I know I'm about to meet strangers: *"Dianne, leave yourself in the car, and go in there to represent me. It's not about you ... it's about Me getting out of you."*

Once the ME is removed from our thinking ... we can burst on the scene with freedom ... and intentionality. Walks in our neighborhood announce our arrival and availability.

Prayer before our walks opens our eyes to potential mission spots. We need God to open our eyes to the potential out there. Oh, the people are there, but often we don't see them clearly enough to see the possibilities.

Years ago, we lived in a home that was located in a country-like setting. I seldom saw another person from my comfort zone 'inside my house.'

Being "new again" in a new neighborhood, and in a new country, I knew I had to get myself out there and just walk. I was getting too lonely inside.

Even though I didn't feel like it, and since the Welcome Wagon neighbors were not pounding on 'my' door, I'd go out each day, hoping to meet someone with whom I could at least make eye contact with.

God's 'Divine Assignments' usually don't arrive with lights and banners such as: "I'm the one—the stranger whom you'll get to know and love later."

One particular man on my new walk didn't even come with "smile packaging." For weeks we would pass each other. I'd smile and say good morning, and if I recall, he would barely acknowledge my presence.

Stop looking for great facial approval ratings. People burdened with hurts, and many struggles, seldom offer a reciprocal smile.

One afternoon while mowing our lawn, this man whom I'd passed every day for several weeks, approached our house. I never expected any conversation, but to my surprise he came over and said: "Are you aware that you are always smiling when you walk?"

I responded with a surprised and curious look, as I wasn't aware of any facial expression when walking. How we got to the topic of God, I can't remember, but he was the one who brought Him into the conversation.

He asked me if I was a Christian. You know my response without asking – "yes!" He said, "I thought so."

He then proceeded to tell me that his son was a believer, and how his son was praying for him.

Often each person's journey to Jesus is a series of "links in a chain." It was a privilege to be another link in this man's awareness of a Savior who loved him enough to have a stranger greet this man daily with a smile when he was walking.

How we behave and respond to others is representative of the Lord.

I briefly spoke about the joy and pleasure of belonging to a wonderful Lord. I lightly touched on some of God's gracious qualities and left it at that. I guess I couldn't help but smile.

That was about it! From that day on, he would smile and respond every time we saw each other.

There are many, many other people that I've come to know, love and befriend in a similar manner as this man. One conversation leads to another, and on and on it goes.

Had I remained in my home, I would have missed the joy of knowing, loving and learning from dozens of people. No wonder the Lord wants us to come out of our comfort zone … so that we can see the difference He makes just with our "smiles and hello's" along the way.

Looking through the Lens of . . .

Is there a potential friend in your neighborhood you haven't yet met?

Downtown Friendships – Part 1

What continually thrills me is that God can take our *'efforts in the ordinary'* and create them to be extraordinary…for His purposes.

Here is one such example.

At various times during our lives, God has called my husband to an overseas assignment. For me, it was a more 'local operation,' only three blocks from our downtown condo.

It is amazing that God delights in the *'simple details'* of our lives. I love the fact that what may be 'ordinary,' is actually very exciting.

I say that, because somehow our Father carries out His plans right *'in those details.'* We never know "where or how" He will work and carry us to places to fulfill His plan in the "lives of others."

When God parked us downtown to live in a condo, we had only one car. So, if I wanted to go out shopping or for a walk, I would have to use the #11 bus (my legs).

I'm painting a picture here for a reason. We were new in a new town, and I knew no one. I am a people-person, and now without transportation, how do I meet and make new friends. I'm thinking: "God, You're aware of all this."

One morning I was desperate for some kind of interaction with people, so I decided to go out for a walk. I didn't want to venture too far—just a few blocks and back again until I learned the lay of the land.

In other places we've lived, my focus on meeting my neighbors was to bake cookies or cake and share whatever I made with them. People always seem to open their door to food.

Now, I'm hitting the streets looking for people to just say "hello" to and hope for future conversations and possible friendships.

I'm thinking that this is highly unlikely, as who's going to make friends with strangers on the street??? But that's without taking **"God into account."**

On my walks every morning and afternoon, I would see and make eye contact with about nine people. Some were street vendors; artists; fortune tellers; jewelry designers; a man who (very cleverly) balances rocks; as well as a guy who enjoys alcohol ... a lot; and one woman with a bag open soliciting donations for food.

During my first few excursions, I *wrongly assumed* that there wasn't anyone with whom I had anything in common. I would take the same route each morning as I walked our two little dogs.

I'd see the same kaleidoscope of faces, and by week number three, I had their 'locations memorized.'

My street contacts now know that I too am a 'regular.' Even the dogs got to recognize our regular acquaintances and knew when to stop. By now we're all comfortable with our "hellos" to each other.

After about six weeks of this, and still desperate for a friendship of some kind ... God gives me the idea of baking banana bread and sharing it through the week with these nine people.

Some of them were easy to share with. Others I just kept at a smile's distance away for a while, and for wise reasons. On the street I learned, you 'earn trust and a rapport.'

One morning, as I was approaching this woman, who waves and says "hello" to everyone that walks past her, I received a 'heart nudge' from the Lord to share a piece of banana bread with her and ask her name.

In the past, I avoided looking at her when I walked by. Oh, how awful of me! I would never have thought I was prejudiced, but the Lord pointed out graphically that my body posture told another story.

The following morning, I took several pieces of banana bread that I had in our freezer, and placed them in a bag to distribute to others ... but according to my agenda, this woman wasn't to be one of the recipients. I felt fearful.

She was friendly to others, so it wasn't because she was fearsome to be around. Quite honestly, it was because she was different and I hesitated to have eye contact. I'm so ashamed to admit that, but it was the truth.

Don't you just hate it sometimes when the Lord tells you the truth about your inner attitude, perspective and behavior!

I certainly wasn't "on board with the Lord" about this. But as my heart beat faster, I approached this woman and asked if she would accept a piece of homemade banana bread from me?

Her warm smile and instant "yes" put me at ease. I then asked her name. As soon as she told me, something transpired within my heart! I no longer felt hesitant in her presence, but was overcome with an endearing compassion for her.

This first encounter with her was a step of obedience I will never forget. On the way home, God seemed to quietly whisper to my heart, "Thanks for sharing your banana bread with Me!!"

Within weeks, this woman whom I had *ignored* for some time, agreed to go to church with my husband and me every Sunday. She told me where she lived (above a tavern in the downtown area), and we agreed on a time that we would come by and pick her up. This went on for almost two years.

I can honestly say that my general features and appearance don't usually attract a crowd, even on a good day. My friend walks with a limp and we were arm-in-arm as we approached the church. As we walked through the patio of the church, we felt eyes turning toward us.

Perhaps because she's a little over 6 feet tall, and I'm just 5' 2," and as we entered the church, we had an entire coliseum of eyes upon us.

That first Sunday, I felt a little awkward. I should add that her attire was extremely casual, and I had chosen to dress "down" a bit, for her benefit.

I was disappointed that the man greeting at the door wasn't as friendly to us as he was to the other people coming through the doors. He did however, shake our hands, but that was about it.

I'm thrilled to say that after about four weeks of our attending this church, he began to smile and greet us both more warmly (if you know what I mean).

One Sunday soon after that, while my friend was seated in the sanctuary, I went back out to the door and shared with the gentleman how I met my new friend, and to tell him why she was coming. This is important for you to know … as things began to change.

The following week the Lord prompted me to take my friend to a Walmart and flood the cart with some new clothes for her – new shoes, tops and slacks, and a pair of earrings.

I knew she must have felt a little awkward with her attire, and I thought it was important that she be able to relax as she adjusted to her new surroundings … a church!

During this time, I began introducing myself and my new "city friend" to others where we'd sit each week at church. Each week the people that we sat around began to greet and be especially friendly to my new-found friend.

Slowly the greeters at the door began to smile at her too and even give her hugs. *I wonder if they ever realized that God was hugging this woman "through their arms."*

As time went along, she felt so loved and accepted, just like it's supposed to happen when believers are together. Remember Jesus takes all of us, *just as we are!*

"Suppose a man or woman comes into your meeting wearing gold ring and fine clothes, and a poor man or woman in shabby clothes also comes in. If you show special attention to the man wearing fine clothes and say, "Here's a good seat for you," but say to the poor man, "You stand there" or "Sit on the floor by my feet," have you not discriminated among yourselves and become judges with evil thoughts?" James 2:2-3

The Sunday after our shopping spree, a rather tall, nice-looking, well-dressed young woman, approached our car ... *IT WAS HER!!!* She looked stunning.

I couldn't believe the change. She even carried herself smartly. I think she grew an inch in height being so proud of her new and fresh appearance.

Then it happened, I felt as though I was going to be overcome with tears of emotion. Instantly the Lord presented a "sermon of His heart" to me as she approached the car. So now would be a good time for me to include for you, God's little epistle to me that morning.

He didn't need to address me by name, I "knew" who He was talking to – me.

He unraveled the truth of what He did for me when I first gave my life to Christ: He dressed me in new clothes–His righteousness. Then, this new inner nature that He gifted me with, was more "attractive" than how I used to be; and now, this new nature within me would draw others to His presence.

What a difference Christ makes when we're "dressed in Him" and "by Him." Our new wardrobe draws others to Him (or at least that's how it's supposed to be).

I never wanted to openly display my emotions, but she was delighted that I noticed and expressed how pretty she looked.

Now, let me share the exciting part. By the fifth week, the greeter at the door gave us both a hug. Yes, I said hug. The kind with both arms around you and makes you feel welcomed and loved. This was 1 Peter 2:17 in action! "Respect everyone, and love the family of believers…"

After about six weeks, the "steady glances" we received when we arrived at church stopped, and a few genuine smiles began to appear. Why, one would have thought that we had been attending that church for years!

One woman who sat close by even brought new clothes for my friend as well. And then at Christmas, she wrapped some money in a Christmas card for my friend too.

I'm continuing to believe that **LOVE IS MORE CAUGHT THAN TAUGHT.** Some people even came up to say hello to us from where they were sitting.

It was such a thrill to see God in action…. right there in church!!!! My friend will never forget those experiences of God's love toward her.

Then after church, before I'd take her home, we would go to McDonalds drive-through for a couple of dollar chicken sandwiches. Gosh, that sounds good to me right now.

Downtown Friendships – Part 2

The following two years of walks brought me to a point of having a *"clearer vision"* and a *"warmer heart"* for these nine new friends. You see, God wanted me to begin the learning process of seeing people with *His eyes, and with His heart.*

Though we can see things with our eyes ... but not always with our hearts.

I could share for hours, but I want to talk about a few other street stories.

The most difficult relationship for me was the man who enjoyed his alcohol ... too much and on a regular basis. He would sit slumped over or be asleep on the sidewalk.

For months, I'd not only look away, but I would walk as far away from him as possible.

You can probably guess the next lesson the Lord had in mind for me to learn. God was now extending my refreshment offerings to include him as well. It took about four months of giving "banana bread" on a daily basis to him, before he'd even say any more than a quiet "thanks."

Another few months passed, and I slipped him a letter with my story of how I came to realize I needed Christ, along with his banana bread. The next day he told me that he kept my letter.

Another few weeks passed and he announced, "Tomorrow is my birthday."

What a breakthrough. He finally felt "safe enough" with me to expose a window into his heart, a heart that was hurting and needed a loving touch.

Some friends were visiting us at the time, and when we all went out walking, I shared about my new friend and that tomorrow was his birthday. We all thought it was a good idea that we take a "birthday party to him."

I asked our friends if they would like to come along for my daily walk, and they were thrilled to be invited.

That morning we gathered some banana bread, and wrapped some new underwear and socks and included a nice card.

Over to the park we travelled to surprise our friend. If I remember correctly, we approached him that morning all singing HAPPY BIRTHDAY.

He smiled from ear to ear. We presented the gift, goodies and card and he was clearly delighted.

After some conversation and introduction to our visiting friends, we turned to walk away, when I noticed one of our friends slipping him another gift. It was a "green folded gift." How loving was that ... and oh so needed.

This *come-as-you-are-party* was his *last birthday on earth.*

Months later, due to illness, he was taken off the streets and placed in a safe home. I've been told by another woman, who gave toiletries to the people in this area, that she worked to get him into a group home setting for his care.

She kept in close contact with him and shared with me that he was changing and, that he had become a Christian.

This guy had been rejected by his family and so many others all his life. Though I couldn't see my new friend any more, I phoned him through the week and sent hello cards to him.

He wasn't rejected by God, but as a prodigal, was welcomed home. God is "more than amazing."

I remember my last conversation with him that took place by phone one evening, and the next day the Lord took him home to a brand-new place ... a place in heaven prepared just for him.

Another opportunity I must share about is an episode with Ravi (the man who balances rocks). It was Christmas Day and he was building his arrangement of rocks for the many onlookers. Dozens of people were gathered around him. I came over to smile and wave and to introduce him to my husband.

When he saw me, he stopped his entertainment and came over to talk to me. I knew from his countenance; something was terribly wrong. He blurted out," My dad died this morning."

Crowd or no crowd, this man needed a hug. Right then and there I took hold of his hands and began to pray for him. We both ignored his captivated audience and turned our hearts heavenward. That day our friendship was sealed.

Later I brought over a plate of turkey and all the trimmings for his dinner as he was working all day and just had a sandwich in his bag. It was Christmas Day!

God is showing me, through these people—these new friends, *"new graces of outreach."* I'm loving the lessons, and even though I'm a slow learner, at least I'm in the class.

When we first moved into this city, it was about seven weeks before Christmas and we knew no one. I was lonely and feeling a little depressed and so I really wasn't up to an "outreach to anyone."

But I knew God blesses our efforts ... and I needed to just *"make an effort for God to bless."*

I had made some shortbread (see I don't always make banana bread like some of you are thinking), and I thought I'd share a little with one or two neighbors in our condo building.

It was Christmas Eve and we were heading home from a church service. My husband dropped me off at the front door area and drove around and into the parking garage. It took a little time to fiddle around with my keys and open the gate before I could get into the front door.

By the time I was opening the door to go inside, I hear my husband announcing: "We've got company!"

That's impossible I thought as we don't know anyone.

To make a long story short this man and his 23-year-old daughter (who had cerebral palsy) had just arrived with chocolates and a card with Scripture on it. They were our first guests in our small condo for cheese, crackers and some sparkling grape juice.

I shared with them that we'd love to have them stay for a snack, but it wouldn't be fancy as we just arrived home from a church service. We sat down and the first thing he said was: "I'm a Russian Jew."

That comment stopped my heart. These were two people that needed to be loved in a cracker-and-cheese-manner. That encounter began a fruitful friendship. Later, I discovered they enjoyed eating banana bread as well.

Every so often, I would invite them for a lunch on our little patio. Throughout the months, our friendship grew, and about a year later an opportunity opened up for me to give them a Bible.

Being aware of these two lovely people brought such a joy and many opportunities to share about God.

The Lord has introduced me to such a variety of people I would never have thought possible to connect with. They're both my *"teachers"* and my *"treasurers"*. These new relationships are teaching me about reaching out to those who are otherwise ignored.

Some are street vendors with clever abilities. There are a few who are desperate financially and wait for others to demonstrate generosity ... just so they can have enough to eat.

I won't go into great detail, but I sensed God placing in me a magnetic attraction to them; and I can't begin to share how I'm learning fresh avenues of "grace, love and unconditional love" to these dear ones.

The Scriptures are so vivid and alive with the truth of Matthew 6:21: "Wherever your treasure is, there the desires of your heart will also be."

These relationships have become a real treasure to me, and I find such fulfillment in my daily excursions into *their* world, and into *their* hearts.

For many of them, it's taken many months of a smile and a daily hello (followed by sharing banana bread with them) for many of them to accept and trust me.

I've discovered that rich opportunities are often right in front of us. I'm so grateful to the Lord for the surgery on my spiritual vision ... as I began to see people as God does.

My thrill is to be an expression of the love of Christ ... by listening and being a friend. Reaching out in this "city environment" has taken me a <u>way out of my comfort zone,</u> and into the harvest field of others ... *effecting, infecting and reflecting* God's love for them.

I'm amazed at the rapport God is providing me, with them. What a field of harvest God has opened, and a reminder from 1 Peter 2:17: "Respect everyone, and love the family of believers..."

We are surrounded by fields ripe for harvest ... but oh the need is for us to get *"into their arenas of living ... in their field, on their turf ... and where they live, and to look for practical ways to touch their lives, and let them know they're special and loved by their Creator."*

We all face a vast array of circumstances and seemingly impossible situations that when fully understood become great opportunities.

So That's Your Favorite Color!

Women are probably more attuned to another woman's style and hair cut than men don't you think?

When we women get together with friends for company and conversation, we notice the little details about others. Such observations encourage and build a better bond with our friends.

If we're honest, we'd have to admit how often we have been more concerned about how <u>our</u> shoes match, or that the color *we* wear accent our features.

However, it's the "inner beauty" of a person that makes a person really attractive.

We are God's masterpiece, because He fashioned us in our mother's womb. This knowledge that God designed each of us personally and intimately makes us special to Him and should make us very secure.

Secure people know that the tags on our clothing don't ever determine our identity or status. These people know who they are, and are easily able to compliment others.

I can almost count on one hand the number of sincere compliments I've received from other women. I often tease other gals when I've complimented them by saying: "If another woman says you look pretty, *you look pretty*."

This wee story isn't to solicit sincere compliments. Rather, it is a lesson in the practice in the "observation of others." To value another person does, of necessity, require us to forget about our self and *focus on the other individual*.

For getting the mail, my routine is to usually head right for the mailbox, and straight back to the house, because I usually have things I need to do. I seldom chat with anyone on the street when doing this.

One morning as I walked out to get the mail, I noticed my neighbor in her front yard. I walked across and said "hello" as I seemed to catch her eye. It was as though my steps seemed to pause and turn around in the middle of my return to our home. I had a busy schedule that morning, and I wasn't in a chatty mood—you know: *things to do; places to go; people to see.*

My goal was just to retrieve the mail and get back to my busy life.

This morning however, in my mailbox marathon, my feet traced their steps into her yard. That wasn't *my plan* ... but spontaneity (and the sovereignty of God) moved me in that direction.

What I hadn't realized that morning is that God "is into the details" of our life.

This lovely neighbor lady is customarily dressed in casual jeans but I "happened" to notice that she had on a lovely green sweater, and as I looked, I became curiously focused on her ears.

Though not my usual scan-pattern when I meet people, but that morning my eyes were drawn from her sweater to her ears.

You're wondering where I'm going with this? Stay tuned, there's more coming.

I enjoy building friendships. But it takes a real "push from the Lord" for me to *come out of my personal comfort zone and "forget about myself."* That's the hurdle God wants all of us to succeed in crossing.

On Thursdays, I usually pray for all the neighbors surrounding our home. I had been asking the Lord for a growing sensitivity to notice people, and to know "how to reach out in practical, yet personal ways."

Later that week I was shopping (something I'm not fond of doing–really!!), and I passed by a jewelry counter and noticed some expensive pierced earrings on sale. Since, I don't wear pierced earrings ... there was no need to pause by that counter.

Yet, a pair of green earrings seemed to shout "take me home." They also happened to be the very shade of green as in my neighbor's sweater ... the one she wore the other day.

It wasn't important that she was wearing a nice sweater. What *was important* is that "someone noticed ... really noticed her." This kind of observation "honors another" because it shows that we're interested in a person, and that they aren't just a "backdrop" to our day.

Well, the earrings popped into my purse ... after I paid for them of course, and they were assigned for my neighbor.

I brought them home and wrapped them in a little box. It wasn't long before I made my way over to her home. It wasn't Christmas or her birthday, but just an average day. A great day to give an "unexpected gift" to an "unsuspecting neighbor."

Her response was incredible, as I learned two things about her. First, her favorite color was green, and second, she asked, "how did you know I had pierced ears?"

Here was an "everyday encounter" in which God sensitized me to "notice others" ... and the target He used was my neighbor across the road.

That observation and my response to God's leading, opened a door.

GOD IS PRACTICAL ... if we just allow Him to be. WHY?

God can use our eyes to see others: to relate to them; to help them by meeting a need they have; to smile at others, or just to encourage them with a "tiny surprise."

Ask God to let you be on the lookout for people ... as more than just "background material" in the course of the daily steps of your walk each day.

By the way, do you know if your "female friends" wear pierced earrings, or clip-ons? If you do, that's observation!

Guess Who Is Receiving Mail?

Do you know your mailman or mail gal? Perhaps many of you do, but some of you may never have had the opportunity of ever seeing them, because you live in a condo, or in an apartment where your paths never cross.

Some years ago I was a care-giver for my dear mom. The caring routine kept me busy and focused. It was my "joy" to have this opportunity. But one day I was really missing my contact with others outside of our home.

In my quiet time with the Lord that day, I shared with Him that I missed the social and relational time with others. I informed Him that with my care-giving responsibility there seemed to be no one else that I got to talk with or to see.

It didn't take Him long to remind me that I had "overlooked an obvious opportunity." In fact, it was the lady who delivers our mail every morning.

I thought she wouldn't know me if I was on the street. We had never met. How in the world would I make a personal contact with her? God has His ways, and they aren't complicated.

"Write her one sentence on a piece of paper and attach the note to a nice large piece of banana bread." By now I should be recognizing His promptings through the language of food; but I'm still slow in this department of spiritual intuition.

I'm aware that in these days, it's risky to trust a stranger. My first thoughts were, "Do you think this is appropriate? Maybe she doesn't like banana bread. Will she think I'm nuts distributing food on her route?" or "Perhaps Post-Office policies may prevent her from "sampling tastie's out of a mailbox." I guess if she doesn't like it, she can always just leave it in the mailbox.

And my final thought (although this didn't cut any ice with the Lord) was, "We don't know each other." By now you can imagine the Lord's comment back to me. "She'll know you better after you give her the banana bread."

I followed the Lord's suggestion. If I hadn't, I would have missed out on the joy and the subsequent relationship that followed.

Like a hunter, I camped out by the front window all morning, waiting for my mail gal's arrival. She opened the box, and seemingly looked quite surprised. It only took a moment for her hand to reach into the mailbox and remove "mail and a package … for her!"

She peeked up to notice me in the window, and a huge warm smile spread from ear to ear. We waved to each other, and that was the beginning of a lovely, daily "hello relationship."

As time went on, whenever I'd be outside working in the yard, I would try and make sure it was around the time when I knew she would appear … just to say hello. This turned out to be a daily social breath of fresh air for me.

Later, she would often stop and bring packages to my door and we'd chat for a few minutes.

I eagerly looked forward to her daily wave, or smile as she popped our bills and letters into our box. On occasion I'd leave banana bread or cookies in the mailbox for her. She told me later that on her days off, she'd let her replacement carrier know of "unexpected treats," and that they were safe to eat.

It was over a year later that a new mail gal came to deliver our mail. I noticed this for a few days. One day while I was delivering another piece of banana bread in the box, the substitute mail gal came along.

She told me that the other gal would not be delivering mail for a while. She was on a leave-of-absence due to the loss of her son who had taken his life. My heart sank.

I managed to get her home address from her substitute, and wrote her a short note in a nice card.

Weeks later she reappeared on our route and came to my door, and with tears shared about her loss. I told her I would be praying for her and her family.

There was nothing I could "do" ... but I could let her know I cared; and that I cared enough to write a little note.

Have you ever written a "thank you note" to "your" mailman or mail gal? They deliver our mail and, seldom do they receive a note or expression of appreciation from us.

You'll be amazed at what God can do with just a note of encouragement. There were times when I'd just write "thinking of you, and appreciating your service on our behalf."

Please don't be concerned that your "hello" must appear on a nice card. Sometimes I just use a serviette/napkin or a plain piece of paper.

I was certainly aware that, her service was "important," and "expected." But I wasn't up-to-speed in my consideration of her or of what she might experience during the course of her day.

One may think that driving a postal van, or walking up and down streets delivering papers and mail isn't the most thrilling of occupations. But, (and that's a big word) it's an "important service" to everyone.

God has given you and me certain abilities (or gifts) to help others through various means and occupations. No job is more important than another.

Thus, each of us has "something to offer others." God is teaching me that my "gift" is to appreciate the services and kindnesses of people I encounter.

I am sure that if you or I were delivering mail, our work would be much more enjoyable by being surprised occasionally with a treat or a word of appreciation.

If we are to be "lights" in our world because of the "Light of the world within us," I suggest that we change the setting, or turn up the wattage so that we can be seen more clearly by those whose practical services touch our lives on a regular basis.

Want to spread some light? If your mailbox is large enough for a little "goodie" ... try attaching a note to your packaged treat and see what happens.

Your social life may gain one lovely addition.

A 7 AM Latte Delivery

My husband and I resided in a small downtown condo in a large southern California city. Since our unit was on the street level, we saw a variety of people walk past our patio daily. They were a mix of local residents, the homeless, and many visitors from around the world. Had we left the window blinds open, our community resembled a large aquarium ... of people.

My morning routine consisted of taking our two little dogs out on the side patio for a "potty break" every morning around 6:00 a.m. It was not long before I began noticing other peoples' morning patterns and habits. Of course, there was a Starbucks coffee shop just down the sidewalk from our home. Need I say more? I could almost chart the people and times of those who would walk past our place for their morning "cuppa" and off to their employment.

Most of the coffee shop's customers were the general public, but there was one man I noticed whose routine consisted of leaving our building at 6:00 a.m. sharp, and returning about six minutes later with "coffee" in hand.

He seemed a quiet guy, and it was weeks before he even looked up to notice me standing there in my lavender robe with our dogs. Admittedly, my somewhat unmade appearance left a lot to be desired so early in the morning. One morning I took a risk and said, "Hello." He glanced over and replied with a soft, "Hello." That was it.

I would see him in the hall occasionally, but he never seemed to want to make eye contact. All our dwellings in the past were in a home, and routinely I took the initiative to develop some rapport with our neighbors. It only seemed natural that a morning "Hello" seemed in order. However, no matter what I did to make eye contact and say "Hello" to him, it was obvious he was not interested in knowing his neighbors who lived two doors or 19 steps down the hall from him.

I have made it a habit to pray for our neighbors on Thursdays. Since he was a neighbor, I began to pray for him. Part of what I asked the Lord was for an open a door of opportunity to make eye contact, and for our neighbor to feel comfortable saying "Hello."

One day this neighbor was struggling to enter the building from the parking garage. His arms were full of packages, and he was struggling to enter the door without dropping his goods. The Lord provided an opportunity for me to be present, smile and open the door for him.

There it was–a hint of a smile. The following morning at, you guessed it, 6:00 a.m. he began his coffee routine. This morning, though, was different. When returning coffee in hand, he looked over and called out with a stronger, "Hello."

A few days later, again at 6:00 a.m. as he returned from Starbucks, I asked. "Do you like lattes?" Perhaps this was like asking a rabbit if it likes carrots, because he perked right up and said, "Yes, but I never buy lattes at Starbucks because then my daily habit would be too expensive."

Later that day I put a note under his door explaining that we had a latte machine, and my husband and I enjoyed one every morning before he went to work. I also mentioned that the next time he saw me, he could let me know if he would like a latte some morning.

The following morning you can guess what happened. He was on his usual route to that coffee place, and glanced over to where I usually stood, and he brought up the fact that having a latte would be, and I quote, "FABULOUS!" I told him we usually had ours around 7:00 a.m.

We agreed that at 7:00 a.m. the following morning there would be a gentle tap on his front door, and if he looked down upon opening his door, a latte would be placed in a conspicuous spot next to his door.

Strangely, our neighbor did not go to Starbucks the next morning ... because today was the day for the delivery of the "liquid gift." He was likely anxiously waiting ... anticipating ... his first latte delivery.

My husband and I were both up and ready, and the process had begun: latte machine – on; milk–being heated and frothed; bottle of vanilla flavoring–opened. Preparations were complete and it was ready for delivery down the hall.

By now, I had the neighbor's cell number, and sent a short text: "Your latte has been delivered and outside your door." Within minutes he texted back that he was thrilled with his FABULOUS LATTE.

This is how it all began. Sometimes we'd text him to say, "It's on its way," and he'd be standing there waiting for it. As the weeks passed by, we even got into discussion in the halls as he was sipping his latte.

Our deliveries continued about four days a week, which soon turned into months, and we became "liquid friends."

Soon his greetings and smiles in the hall were like a social gathering. My husband and I used to laugh at his texts each time he'd receive a latte. At Christmas time he left a nice gift package at our door.

One morning after his "liquid delivery" he commented that he felt 'spoiled rotten." So, from then on, his nickname became SR for spoiled rotten. His nickname for me is Betty Barista! I can't imagine why?

What a lovely rapport God gave us with this man. I was able to share my story of why I became a Christian and our friendship continues even though we moved away a year or so later.

Our morning deliveries came to an abrupt end when we moved away, and though we're no longer living in that area, we still text from time to time. This man became a dear friend, and we phone him with a question on his birthday each year, "Would you like a birthday latte?"

Every once in a while, I text him and inquire if there have been any liquid latte deliveries at his door. Needless-to-say, it has been a real dry spell at his condo.

Being intentional about reaching out to show care for another has wonderful dividends!! The best is just having him as a friend.

Mathew 5:16 "In the same way, let your light shine before others, that they may see your good deeds and glorify your Father in heaven."

Ephesians 2:10 "For we are God's handiwork, created in Christ Jesus to do good works, which God prepared in advance for us to do."

2 Corinthians 5:20a "We are therefore Christ's ambassadors, as though God were making His appeal through us."

Who Takes in Your Garbage Can?

As I write about this "encounter," I'm almost coming out of my nylons. God is giving me His passion of "living an intentional life," looking for and loving those in my daily walk.

Trust me, in this story I didn't even need to leave my home to experience it.

My mentors on this unique outreach adventure were my parents. My mother would bake each week. At first, we thought she was baking for my dad, but there was another man in her life that was the benefactor of her baking agenda at the beginning of the week.

Each week my parents would be ready for their "garbage guy" as they affectionately called him. My dad's assignment: watch and wait for the garbage truck by perching himself at the living room window. When sighted, he would yell for mom, and she'd bring a brown bag to the front door and wait until the garbage man brought in their trash can.

After he'd bring in their can, he would make a bee-line for their front door where mom would give him the package of homemade goodies—cookies or banana bread or whatever she felt like baking that week.

He would happily hop back into his truck, and the "pick up the garbage guys" continued on to the rest of their neighborhood. One week my dad missed the arrival of the garbage truck. My mom wasn't happy about that. Never mind, they weren't going to get upset about it, but they sure weren't about to have any regrets either.

So, they jumped into their car and drove all over the neighborhood looking for the large green garbage truck – knowing that when they found the truck, they'd find their man! They made the "customary delicious delivery" and returned home. The following week, you guessed it, my dad was much more alert.

The bug bit me ... and I wanted to follow suit wherever we lived. My approach was a little different as I didn't have the time to "watch and wait" for my sanitation engineer's arrival.

I would tie a plastic bag to our garbage can, and I informed our collector that when he saw a bag tied to the can, it was "his goodie bag."

Believe me I could tell you stories of how that's impacted others well beyond the garbage guy. But here's my recent "outburst of joy" that God gave me ... while living in Canada.

In another story, I shared when I was a care-giver for my mom and that our garbage guy wouldn't allow me to bring in our can for years. Since moving to another country, Canada, I wondered what would happen if I did the same thing in another culture.

I discovered that people just love to be loved, irrespective of their address, their cultural, religious, ethnic, or socio-economic background.

I like to refer to my garbage man as my "personal sanitation engineer." We were new in the area, and I watched for his arrival in the big yellow rubbish truck.

They have new trucks now, so the men just pull up to your trash can, and pull or press a lever, and a pair of steel arms protrude out, grab the can, dump the contents into the truck, and place it back at the curb. Because of the new design of the truck, I needed to meet our garbage guy and explain what my plan of action would be for him each week.

The big day arrived, Friday. I paced and peered out my front window waiting for his arrival. Oh, my goodness, who in their right mind WAITS for the arrival of the garbage man? Well, I do, because I wanted to see what GOD WOULD DO with this tiny outreach of the love of Christ.

When he pulled up, I was "ready for him." He saw me parked by the can, and I waved and yelled out that I had something for him. I began to explain my Friday agenda.

He had a look of surprise on his face, but after peering into the bag that this stranger gave him, a smile appeared from ear to ear.

Can you guess what happened next? Yep, he took in my can and hasn't allowed me to take it in since. I went out the following week to bring in the can, but he said that he was going to do that in the future and that I wasn't to touch it.

He does this every week. As I pray for our neighbors every Thursday, this young man has been a lovely addition to that list.

Remember the movie Chariots of Fire, when the runner said "When I run, I feel His pleasure." Well, this is what I feel every week when I attach a goodie bag to our garbage can. I feel such joy that I feel as if I'm going to pop!

Before Christmas the first year, I phoned the company to find out his name. Then just before Christmas, I wrote a long, complimentary letter to his boss about his excellent and contagious attitude, along with a pleasant disposition.

I informed them that this young man's approach and attitude was such an asset to their company and that he was worth his weight in gold. I mailed the letter to this man's supervisor and placed two copies of the letter in his goodie bag.

The following week, when I saw him, (and no I don't wait for him by the window each week) he hopped out of the truck and gave me a big hug. Yes, I wonder what the neighbors think ... but by now I think they've caught on to the goodie bag.

His pleasure at what I did leapt out of his skin, and he let me know that the company gave him a "gift certificate" to a local coffee shop as a little reward for his good service.

One of these days I look forward to sharing Christ with this man, and giving him a copy of my story of why, and how, I became a Christian. When we love others in practical ways, we can say almost anything to them.

Why? Because people know we appreciate them and love them with the love of the Lord in a visual and felt way. Simple, practical actions speak "loudly" of Christ's love to lost souls. We read in Matthew 10:42:

"And if anyone gives even a cup of cold water to one of these little ones who is my disciple, truly I tell you, that person will certainly not lose their reward."

The verse is from Matthew 10:42, and is one of my favorite verses because, like a cup of cold water, God reminds me that <u>**He notices, uses and blesses every tiny little thing we do for others on His behalf.**</u>

This endeavor may never make the news, but tiny little "expressions of grace and care" never miss the eye of our Lord. Oh, the joys of living out the love of God, and continually being a tangible expression of Jesus Christ's love.

Most of the time we all live "ordinary, oatmeal lives." There are no events that would draw attention to a newspaper, it's just everyday living. And in **our everyday**, we have "divine opportunities" sprinkled around us waiting to happen as we reach out with a smile, a hug, a goodie bag or just a look of approval to another.

People are waiting for our 1 Peter 2:17 approach ... they wait to be noticed: "Show proper respect to everyone, love the family of believers, fear God, honor the emperor."

Let's be "intentional" in looking out for our mailman, garbage collector, supermarket checkout clerk, or people we pass on a walk.

We all have "divine opportunities" rather regularly, don't you see that? We just need the lens of our focus, adjusted so that we see others as He does.

We Met in the Parking Lot

It was a cold winter morning. I had just arrived at church and my husband was out of town that weekend. I try and remember to ask the Lord to direct me to just the people He intends for me to meet and interact with each day and today was no exception.

But it happened sooner than expected.

I was a little early, and after parking my car, I made my way to the entrance of the church. The parking lot wasn't exactly overflowing at that moment.

On my way into the building, I noticed a young woman heading in the same direction as me, but I was "on mission" to get into the building.

However, God's Spirit caused me to stop, turn around, and "notice this young gal." She seemed lovely and very friendly.

As I looked at her, I saw that she seemed to have some sort of a struggle in the way she related to me. She appeared to struggle with her words, but her bright smile easily warmed up our conversation.

Searching for conversation, I asked her if she had ever attended here at the church before ... and wouldn't you know it, she said she was "new" and visiting for the first time.

I know "new" first hand. It can be scary and intimidating to enter a place where you know no one, and where there are groups of people interacting together, yet no one speaks or even acknowledges your presence.

Being new, I thought it wise to introduce her to the ladies' room, and then we walked into the sanctuary together. We were both alone, so I took her arm and said, "Let's sit together."

I had no idea of what would take place in that service ... for her ... or for me.

She was new all right; not only to the church, but she was unfamiliar as to how to conduct oneself during a church service. She may have thought it was similar to a movie theater because her own interactions with me throughout the service were totally out of context of where we were.

Bless her heart, she was making comments and asking questions all throughout the service. I moved into a more mothering role, and placed my hands gently over my mouth to suggest she might want to be quiet for a while, but I think she interpreted that as "turn up the volume in her voice."

So I needed to initiate a "shuuu sound," and told her we could talk more after the morning service. People were beginning to notice our presence in a not so complimentary way.

Now at this point of the story, I could just pass over what was brewing in my heart ... but I can't, it wasn't a pretty sight.

For a few minutes I felt like I just couldn't wait until the service was over so that I could excuse myself and tell this young gal with an inquiring mind, that I needed to get home.

The service ended; however, the Lord hadn't finished the sermon instructions for my heart. Gosh, I feel like I'm always in class ... and believe me, this day I needed to be.

Coffee, tea and donuts were served afterwards, and I pointed to the area where she could just help herself to a refreshment.

You can just about figure out what came next in the Lord's Sunday morning agenda for me. Before I could creatively manufacture a way out of this scenario, I found myself escorting her over to the tea and coffee and bought her a donut.

This young woman just needed someone to "pay attention to her and show love to her," even if it felt uncomfortable to me.

Leaving one's comfort zone seems to be a theme in this process of becoming more like Jesus, doesn't it? She shared a little about her life and her needs over tea.

It wasn't long before she had dispatched her donut and finished her tea. Suddenly she was ready to leave. She threw away her cup and out the door she went with a big smile and a goodbye to me.

There had been no indication that our "Sunday rendezvous" was about to end so abruptly.

I had experienced two sermons that morning. One in the sanctuary and the other over tea and a donut. She was my teacher that morning! And I was her student.

This was another required lesson in the "character class" of learning how to express love to a precious young woman whom the crowds weren't drawn to. My heart was shaped more like Jesus' heart that morning ... and I needed that.

The following two Sundays I kept looking for her arrival, but never had the pleasure of ever seeing her again. She however, forever changed how I look at the "scenery of people" arriving in the parking lot.

That morning, God was placing me next to my sermon ... someone who wore a lovely smile, especially after a donut and a big hug goodbye.

Portable Commode: "Johnny-On-The-Spot"

Is your imagination getting the best of your curiosity? This little vignette is from when we lived in a condo, and our unit was just steps from the trash bin room.

I wouldn't admit to being a dumpster diva, but for the record, I did keep a vigilant eye on "treasures" that people would part with and deposit in that room.

I was shocked at the nice things people were throwing away. Some of the things were like new, and from other stories you've read, you'll know by now that many of these precious finds went on to my street friends.

I'm not going to fill you in on all the many items I transferred from the trash room into our condo, but there is one worth sharing. You guessed it, the like "new" portable commode.

When my husband came home from work that evening, I had conveniently left it parked in the foyer of our little condo. My purpose in leaving it there was to sanitize it, and then burst with enthusiastic thoughts at its future potential.

My husband wasn't as keen on its potential as I was, but it was so well crafted and detailed in its design, that I knew it would help someone, sometime, somewhere.

Our condo was small, and we had to take it downstairs to our 4' x 6' storage area. My poor husband could not help but share his disgust all the way down the elevator and hallway, and then having to put this "thing" in our storage area for everyone to see.

Our storage area was so full, that we had to toss it up on top of the other boxes and hope for the best.

Months and months went by without a need. Then, the day came. A lovely neighbor many doors down the hall had fallen down a flight of stairs. She was still in agony – having just returned to her condo after staying in the hospital for days.

Her husband was out of town, and she had a friend stay with her until her husband could return from a business trip.

We had heard about her fall and her condition and I contacted her friend in the afternoon, and went over that evening to visit her with a casserole in hand. My neighbor shared her story and as she did, her needs began to unfold.

I looked around and thought about all she had shared with me. There was one specific area of need … she could remain on only one floor. How would she get to a bathroom for "refreshment and the urgent" routine for her personal needs?

She told me she needed her friend to be there all the time to escort her up some steps to get to the bathroom. It was a painful experience just trying to lift herself from step to step.

Idea! Idea! The portable potty would be perfect for her needs for the coming months of healing. YES, I said to myself. I have the perfect solution. As I shared my solution with enthusiasm, my neighbor sighed and cried with relief knowing I had such a portable helper.

It took me 15 minutes to locate the potty and bring it to her condo. Being well designed, it could adjust for any size, and height. Isn't that exciting? I couldn't wait until my husband came home from work to share the news.

Yes, God can use anything to bless another's' life. This "portable potty chair" opened up a number of discussions about Christ.

My neighbor just couldn't be more pleased and relieved (good word here) that her needs were being met.

I also was able to share how I had been praying for her for months prior. Tears of appreciation just rolled down her face. She was a happy camper and God got the glory.

Just Checking in to Say Hello

One of my greatest joys after I was married and moved to Canada was being my precious mom's care-giver. It was never my privilege of living in close proximity to my parents—we were always at least 2,000 miles away.

Since my husband traveled often, his accrued air miles came in handy, and I would make trips to Ohio to visit my parents and help with things to do around their home.

Years later, I experienced a difficult and emotional season after my dad suffered a severe stroke, and eleven days later, he moved to heaven leaving my mom to continue her journey alone in her home.

This was her wish at the time, but two years later she began having serious health challenges.

It was then we invited her to come and live with us. What a joy and privilege that was for us, and she was happy and relieved that she wouldn't need to live alone.

God used my dear mom as an example about loving others in "practical ways." Over the years I observed her daily routine of phoning her own mother just to check in on her.

When I was younger, we lived overseas and she was not able to call daily, but she wrote her mother once a week, without fail. In fact, for about 31 years, my mother wrote me a letter once a week, without fail … just to say hello "in writing." Let me insert here that I enjoy using email like most people, but honestly, I miss "real mail." You know, the envelopes that appear in your mail box with a "handwritten note" tucked inside.

Oh, let's introduce that back into the marketplace and written on our personal agenda.

Growing up included many "moving adjustments." Since dad was in the service, we moved every two years or so. After my dad's retirement, our family settled in one place and they soon began to meet and enjoy longer-lasting neighbors.

When my father could no longer drive, a neighbor, who lived only a short distance away, would come by almost every morning, to take dad to their local grocery.

It was not uncommon to see the two of them parading up and down the aisles. Their frequent trips to the stores allowed them to memorize most of the grocery prices as a result.

This lovely neighbor became a wonderful friend over the years. His wife had passed away, and he felt lost for a long time, but he and my dad connected for their daily trips to the grocery, post office, or wherever either of them needed to make an errand-journey.

I hadn't noticed it at first, but whenever I would go to visit, I saw my mother phone this man every morning. Though he lived a 3-minute drive from my parents, my mom would phone him "just to say hello" and see how he was doing.

Whenever he'd come by in the car, my dad would be sent out with a homemade treat for him, and off they would head for an excursion to a local supermarket. This went on for over fifteen years.

Her daily example of this **"practical love"** was incredible. Her daily conversations weren't long, perhaps only 5 minutes or less. But when I asked why she did that, she responded by saying, "I just wanted to check up on him because he was alone."

God used **"her pattern of loving"** to help me catch a glimpse of God's heart for others, especially those who are alone, or are going through a difficult time. We've all been there, or will walk that path one day.

When widowed years later, and due to health issues, she came to live with us. Almost all of my time was spent in caring for her needs. My husband's job took him away from home Monday through Thursdays, and I was alone in my care-giving role.

Now living in our home, over 2,000 miles from her neighbor-friend, my mom continued to phone him daily. Again, her life was speaking volumes on how to look out from 'your life' into the 'life of another.'

The Lord was about to introduce me to a "quiet ministry" to others. I refer to it as "Care Calling!"

It's not a well-known or advertised ministry, but I know from experience the emotional oxygen and encouragement that was infused within me when I would receive a caring call while alone— caring for my mom.

Being alone so much, I came to realize the value of a phone call. The Lord brought two lovely women into my life to help me with my needs. Bless them both.

I am so grateful for their practical, and especially their emotional support. These two women would either call or come over every week just for a visit.

When my dear mom moved to heaven, my "care-calling-clientele" emerged. I took over the task of calling my parent's neighbor friend.

Once I started, I couldn't stop. He often told me how he looked forward to those morning or evening calls.

It is only when you've experienced what it means to give continued care to someone you love, that you can understand the emotional pain, separation, and underlying stress and concern in this loving journey of care. Though you love them immensely and want to do your best, there are times when you are house-bound due to the level and type of care required.

My husband and I had been friends with a lovely man for over twenty years; but it was only when he became the care-giver for his wife, did our daily call routine emerge.

Our hearts began to knit together more closely as we shared his daily journey through our phone calls. Sometimes I would phone in the morning, or in the evening, and we'd talk about what we prepared for dinner or lunch and discuss the happenings of our day ... the good, the bad and the hard things.

We both agreed that our calls were like a life-line of support for one another. These daily calls went on for years, but the day came when he became ill and was placed in Hospice Care.

He was not a believer all those years, but I would gently share my faith. I am convinced that it's our *"life of loving them" and "prayer"* that opens the door to share our faith with others.

It's much easier to talk about the gospel, than to "be the gospel." But when our lips and life are somewhat parallel, the Lord opens many doors of opportunity.

There will always be "goodbye" days, and they are so hard. This new goodbye would be especially difficult because he was the friend who was the care-giver for his wife.

Now he had cancer and was not doing well in the hospital. I phoned the hospital for my daily "hellos" to him.

Just two weeks prior to his being hospitalized, my husband had shared with our friend how the Lord, in answer to prayer, had spared his life ... and was waiting for him to respond to God's call on his life, and wanting to save him and bring him into God's presence.

Who knew that when I phoned this day, it would be on his last day on earth. His daughter answered the phone and I asked to speak to him. He was unable to return any words to me, but I shared with Him that this was indeed a good time to surrender his life to Christ.

I prayed for him on the phone and his daughter said he nodded his head in agreement. I had shared gently, cautiously and lovingly about our need for a Savior for a good number of years, and He knew that my husband and I both loved him and were concerned for his soul.

I'll need to wait until the Lord calls me home to see the reality of all that went on in that last conversation. To my knowledge, I was his only friend that knew Jesus Christ, and for the last time, I introduced him to His own need of a Savior.

Matthew chapter 6 verse 21: "Where your treasure is, there your heart will be also."

When these two "telephone friendships" ended, my heart felt a tremendous void. Our conversations seldom lasted more than five or ten minutes at the most, but the personal and emotional void was ever present.

I feel there have been so many times when the Lord was sharing His heart about others with me, but I missed it. I usually came up with the idea that I had to do **BIG THINGS** for God. But God isn't looking for the big things.

God yearns that we "tune in to His heartbeat for people" in the **LITTLE THINGS** ... that can be **HUGE** in another person's arena of life.

Soon God was about to introduce me to His next significant Care Client–a precious woman who used to team up with me and some other lovely friends in hosting a weekly Bible Study.

My friend felt it was an honor to make tea and coffee every week. Her face and heart seemed to glow as she prepared the liquid refreshment every week for the ladies attending the study.

Some weeks earlier I had learned of the "home-going" of her husband of over fifty years. The Lord planted within me the desire to begin phoning her every morning or evening.

You can just imagine the "rest of the story." We spoke every day for over two years.

Yes, again the pain of the loss of another daily friend began to emerge. Each of these people were my TREASURES! They still are.

I feel like a very rich person ... because God has continued to bring a good number of people along my path to interact with day-by-day, until He calls them home.

Though not a popular ministry, it is a "quiet and powerful ministry" to purposely involve myself in the lives of people: their hurts; their prayer concerns; their joys and their very personal fears.

There was a wonderful book I read after my mom 'went Home' to be with Jesus that gave voice to my emotions. It's called, "May I Walk You Home" by Melody Rossi. I recommend it highly.

We all need others to hold us, talk with us, love us, listen to us, pray with us ... **people that God could use to walk others Home!**

May I suggest that you talk with God and inquire from Him whom He might want to place on your "care-calling" heart?

Just think what a difference a three-minute call every day, or even just a couple times a week to just "check in to say hello" can make in the life of someone.

You'll never know until eternity how critical your calls will be. Yes, you can phone me anytime!

The Gift of Refreshment

This story brings tears to my eyes because my heart recalls the precious friend God brought to me in a big yellow passenger van. We enjoyed friendship with one another for only a short season, about a year and a half; but our "divinely orchestrated" days were filled with eternal memories.

Upon our introduction, my friend shared that she was legally blind; and at our first encounter she wanted me to know that she was unable to see me clearly, and would always require my help in guiding her steps along the way. She was marvelously agile with her "walker," and I always had to keep in step with her or she would be way out in front of me.

I would await her arrival at church via a taxi bus each Sunday morning. She would gleefully exit with the help of the driver, and I would call out her name to let her know I was waiting for her.

After our friendship was sealed, I would phone to check up on her from time to time. We just felt so "at home" with each other. One day I phoned to surprise her with an invitation to join me for breakfast at a fast-food restaurant called Tim Hortons. In her 90 plus years of life, she had never been to this restaurant, nor had she ever tasted an egg and sausage croissant (one of life's little pleasures).

I knew this social outing needed to happen and soon, so a day and a time was chosen in my calendar. When I went to pick her up, she wasn't hard to locate at her assisted living facility. She was waiting front and center in the lobby–standing beside her walker, beaming with anticipation for this up and coming "breakfast surprise." She continued to smile from ear-to-ear while she gleefully consumed that egg and sausage croissant.

She was moved to a nursing home after a fall in her assisted living apartment. Her new room was very sparse, with only a few photos and a cherished quilt that covered her tiny frame. Our weekly visits were precious and joy-filled, and we enjoyed being together either in her room, or out on the patio in the sunshine.

Week after week we would talk together about her wishes for a really "nice" room. Her name was on the waiting list, but it would be months before that move was about to take place. But we made it a matter of prayer.

Every month she seemed to grow weaker and less interested in her "room request." But over a cup of coffee, we'd laugh and chat and exchange a big hug at the end of our time together. She never complained.

Then the big day came! On my next visit I was informed that she was in her "new" room. It was clean and fresh, and her whole being was engulfed in the filtered sunshine that flooded her room.

The visit that day was different ... and she was different. Though she knew someone was there, I wasn't sure that she knew that it was me.

A tender touch is a wonderful kindness to give someone, especially if they can't bring you into focus. Her eyes were dim and so was her countenance. I thought to myself, "What can I do?" It turned into a prayer. I took her hands and just held them, and told her I was there and that she wasn't alone.

I asked if she wanted anything. Her immediate response framed my favorite Scripture. She said she wanted water. I went to a refrigerator for ice and prepared a cold glass of water and inserted a straw. Gently holding the straw to her mouth, she drained the glass and asked for more.

She managed a gracious smile and then shared the sweetest encouragement a soul could hear. "Thanks for being here, and being my friend."

We just held hands while our hearts connected in spirit. My heart just knew that this would be my last opportunity to minister to my sweet friend: and to do so in the fashion of my favorite verse from Matthew 10:42: "And if you give even a cup of cold water to one of the least of my followers, you will surely be rewarded."

Her friendship rewarded my heart many times, and yet I had no idea that this last "gift of refreshment" given to her, would embrace a verse I loved and cherished. A few days later, God took her home to be with Him ... in her "new room" prepared just for her. He not only answered her prayer for a new "earthly room" but He gifted her with His presence, in her new eternal home.

I've discovered that God notices, uses, and blesses our every tiny outreach to others. A glass of cold water is odorless, colorless and tasteless; yet it brings refreshment like none other.

God "gifts our lives" with other people for a myriad of reasons and for special seasons. May we all be encouraged to be sensitive and alert to the "cups of cold-water opportunities" God brings to accompany our walk in life.

Fireplace Dining at a Very Tiny Table!

Do you have a "mentor?" Many wonderful people have mentored me in my life as a woman, wife, friend, and follower of Jesus Christ. The dictionary beautifully defines a mentor as: "A wise and trusted friend, coach, counselor, adviser, an influential supporter."

We had been married for about a year, and as newlyweds, we moved to Calgary, Alberta, Canada. This was a new culture to me, and I did my best to absorb the new and somewhat different way of doing things.

A lovely lady at our church invited me to her home for lunch. I didn't know her well at all, but admit that I admired her from afar.

I loved the fact that this sweetheart of a woman was consistently friendly and inclusive to anyone in her presence.

She had that unique ability to make you feel as though you were the *only one on earth* present when around her.

My husband and I had enjoyed her "creative talents" in the kitchen several times. She could serve bread and butter as though it was a delicacy.

One day, she invited me – just me – for lunch. This is relevant because she usually invited many guests for lunch or dinner, and all of these gatherings were fun, just plain fun.

This invitation to lunch by my new, and soon-to-be friend, was much anticipated.

It was a COLD day when I arrived at the door, and as soon as I entered, I was warmed being enfolded by loving arms in an atmosphere of acceptance and joyful laughter – all of which I shall never forget.

From the doorway, she angled me to the right into a little bedroom that had hosted many coats, purses and sweaters of visitors. I remember just being lost in the sweetness of the room.

It was like visiting a country boutique. Dolls, flowers and antique-like nick nacks were creatively placed all over the room.

Honestly, I could have browsed there for 15 minutes just taking in the ambiance and beauty of the room. It was delightful.

After taking off my coat and receiving another hug, we entered the living room. I can still remember the emerald green carpet and radiant warmth of the flooring under my feet.

The fireplace was in full roar and then … there it was.

A small table draped in a gorgeous white lace–like tablecloth, adorned with fine china, stemmed water glasses, lit candles, and silverware that seemed to sparkle.

The serviette/napkin was so pretty, I hesitated to unfold this masterpiece.

Now I've been over to many homes for lunch, but believe me, this table arrangement and the placement in front of the fireplace was fit for a "Queen!"

I could barely respond to our introductory chit-chat while gazing around the room. On the fireplace mantle were dozens of framed photographs of her family, each attractively placed side-by-side.

She invited me to sit down and be warmed up by the fire as she would soon be bringing in lunch.

When I was growing up, my sister and I were never allowed to eat in the living room. (And we all know why, don't we!)

So this "dining decor" was an incredible way to say I love you, and don't worry if you drop something on the carpet.

She appeared from her kitchen with a tray of delights. The selection included three tea sandwiches, with fruit and scones.

Everything was attractively "arranged" on the plate, almost as if Better Homes and Gardens had commissioned the display.

In contrast, I thought about a lunch experience from my kitchen which would consist of egg salad, lunch meat, or cheese between two slices of bread which I would lovingly call a sandwich.

To my friend, even my meager offering would have been treated as a delicacy, and she would have taken the time to enjoy every morsel.

I noticed that she had removed the crust off each slice of bread and delicately placed a variety of fillings on the runway of the smooth-textured bread. Even the fruit had a special touch.

I could almost imagine her conversing with the strawberry to get its permission to be sliced ever-so-gently at an angle. Can I assume you'd be interested in having lunch with her at this point of my story?

As I was relaxing in this exquisite surrounding, I couldn't help but notice the fireplace blazing with joy. I say joy because my friend was oozing with joy as she shared how special it was for her ... that I was there with her.

Believe me, the joy was all mine.

We must have sat there for almost two hours. I couldn't count the number of cups of tea. We chatted and laughed the entire time.

I never remembered being invited anywhere where everything was just so delicately chosen and arranged ... just for me.

I felt so honored, pampered, and special. I was amazed at her ability to make me feel as though I was the most precious person on earth.

She certainly wasn't without family responsibility, because she was the mother of three children and busy in the lives of many other people.

I recall that she spoke very little about herself. Instead, she wanted to know all about me, who I was, what I enjoyed doing, how my life was being lived.

Today, was *"my day,"* specially planned by her so I would know and feel God's love and her love too. Her presence, laughter, acceptance, love and loving conversation made me feel like royalty.

Our conversation was so inviting and accepting, and when she spoke of others, it was bathed in kindness.

Her laughter was contagious.

I always thought that if she had to correct me in any way, that I'd hardly realize it because of the tenderness that would encompass her every word.

I dared not make a comment about how lovely something was, because I believe she'd have given it to me.

This delightful lady encouraged me to just have "fun with another" … with no other agenda than to show how special they are!

You don't need fine china to do that.

She taught me that I can slap two pieces of bread together, cut out shapes, or tear away the crusts, and place absolutely anything between them.

She taught me that crackers, cheese and a "cuppa' tea" around any size table can make others feel special.

I learned that it's not the menu that makes a lovely luncheon, but the love of the Lord, laughter, and a little table simply adorned with a tablecloth and placed in front of a fireplace, or window.

She was so loving and caring to me that I think I'd have enjoyed lunch even if it was in her bathroom.

This beautiful friend's life, then and now, continues to inspire me in special ways. We no longer live in Calgary, but her loving calls every so often, brighten my spirit.

This dear one will always hold a precious mentoring spot in my life.

During my life many other women have also demonstrated, in diverse ways, how I can bless others by showing them how unique and special they really are!

How thankful I am to God for weaving this wise and winsome woman along my life's journey. She is so gifted in the skill of practical love and outreach, and my life is richer for it.

Thank you Anne, for showing me the love, kindness and generosity of our Lord Jesus. You are one SPECIAL WOMAN, and a lovely forever friend.

How Are You ... Really?

Each day we never know whose steps will interact with ours. My joy and privilege were to greet people who came into our church. This was such a delight for me.

I yearn that my life, in some small way, creates a compelling environment to help people grow closer and deeper in their love and knowledge of Jesus Christ; and, to "be" the "tangible expression of Christ." Or, if they haven't yet developed a personal relationship with Him, they begin to do so ... and so that this becomes reality for them.

My prayer is that through joyfully greeting each person, that I would be able to express their "significance to God" through a smile, a touch, or a word. I wanted them to know before they ever sat down in the church building, that they had been touched by God's love and acceptance.

A compass truth that God has been working into my life is this:

"After people spend time with me, what do they think of Jesus Christ?"

People have often asked me how I can be so friendly to others when, I'm usually the "new" person. God spoke to my heart about this issue, since I have been in many new surroundings, and being the new person much of my life.

But what has God impressed upon me when I walk into a new setting is:

"Dianne, leave yourself in the car!"

That's the key. As for greeting others on Sunday, I'm to leave myself: my fears, my agenda, my needs in the car, and go in and "represent Jesus Christ" to every heart coming through the doors. Each handshake can be a prayer for that person.

I noticed people who lingered just a little longer for a warm handshake, a smile, and an acknowledgement that they are so special to God. God wants to welcome them, through little personal ways, letting them know that He is "so glad they are there."

I want to share two encounters that have refreshed my heart as I employed this practical outreach.

I woke up one Sunday morning a number of years ago in a "not so good frame of mind." I just didn't feel very "welcoming" this particular Sunday. But, thanks to the Lord, I went anyway.

I always feel visitors need a special touch or a hug. A widow arrived at the front entrance of the church. As this lady approached me this morning, I gave her a hug, and then, prompted within, pulled her close again for a longer embrace.

Afterwards she looked at me and said these words (please read them slowly):

"Dianne, I needed that extra hug this morning. You are the only one who touches me all week."

What an impact her words had on me that day. We just never know the burdens, anxieties, cares and grief that are encased within the heart and soul of each person we meet.

Just recently, an opportunity to listen, really listen, came upon my life. A man was coming toward the entry to our church lobby, and I noticed that another man had already said the normal welcoming pleasantries: "Hello, and how are you?" But his comment caught my attention: "Do you really want to know?"

Our normal "Hellos" aren't always accurate, are they? They can seem more like a statement than a question. The two of them spoke for a short time and then he came toward me. The week before he had shared that his precious mom who had been hospitalized for many months was not doing well.

I just knew in my heart, that grief was overwhelming him. I didn't start with: "How are you?" this morning? Instead, I just opened my arms and a flood of tears began to flow from him. He continued pouring out his heart for over 30 minutes.

After he had gained some composure, I walked arm-in-arm through the corridors of the church towards the sanctuary, where the church service was well beyond the half way mark in time.

God had already prepared us both for our time together. I was able to briefly share about the passing of my own mother, and what I had felt from this loss. I didn't say much to this man, but my arms and tears embraced his hurt.

He told me later than he appreciated my walking "with him" in his heart-felt grief that morning.

If you've ever experienced "grief" you know, only too well, that there just aren't sufficient or adequate words for a hurting heart.

May you and I be reminded that the next time we ask someone, "How are you?" that we stay around and listen, *really listen* to how they really are?

Those of us who are strong and able in the faith need to step in and lend a hand to those who falter, and not just do what is most convenient for us. Strength is for service, not status. Each one of us needs to look after the good of the people around us, asking ourselves, "How can I help?" Romans 15:1, 2 (MSG)

Come and See Me ... Anytime

You never know how your day will unfold when you start your morning. For those who call God: Father, He has an agenda for His children. We often have no idea of how we are to participate in His plans ... but ... incredibly He "invites" us to join Him daily. More often than not, we see God's hand in our regular intersections with people.

One morning I answered the phone, and there was a friendly voice at the other end. It didn't take long to determine the caller's purpose. The caller was involved in caring for the affairs of his longtime Sunday school teacher who was his mentor when he was in Sunday school.

Though he and my husband had once been work-associates, I felt it strange that he would phone me since we really were not connected at all. I was even more surprised that he wanted to talk with me.

His need became clearer as he described the need of this woman. She was 95 years young, and because of her particular situation, needed to be relocated to our town – 40 miles away from where she currently resided – and near to the caller and his wife.

This couple loved this woman, visited her weekly, and had also taken care of supervising her financial needs. But now that she would be residing in a care facility much further away, it wasn't going to be convenient to just drop in for a visit. The caller was concerned that this dear elderly lady was now going to be alone, and didn't know anyone in her new location.

He wasn't phoning to ask me to visit her. He simply wanted to know if our church – where we were on staff–had a *"Stephen Ministries"* program. Such a program involves people who would support and care for those living in assisted living facilities.

I listened carefully to what he was telling me about this woman and that her need would be for a weekly companion visit. Though we did have this ministry at the church, I wanted to know more about this "loved lady" in order to share the details of her need more carefully with someone who was involved in this outreach.

Sometimes it's very difficult to connect people together without a first-hand, in-person encounter with them. After talking about the various areas describing her personality, interests and background, I began to think aloud with him.

Our conversation was so pleasant and inviting, that idea came to me that I needed to meet this woman so I would have a better idea of who the Lord would have to connect with her.

The caller told me the address of the facility, her name and room number. Turns out, she lived only about 3 miles from our home. I shared that I thought it would be helpful for me to visit her and assess how the connection could be with *"someone else."*

Several days later I drove over to have my first visit. I am occasionally at a loss for words, but a smile and a hello are a great start. When I walked into her room, she was lying in her bed, and was awake.

I introduced myself, and said that we had a "common friend" who had called to let me know that she was new in the area. The conversation with her was one-sided ... as I did all the talking. I didn't know for sure if her lack of speech was due to a stroke, or if it was the medication. She would only mumble in response to my words.

It's so wonderful that the Lord knows just how to orchestrate events and present ideas to us that may seem out of the ordinary. For this first visit, I had brought our 7-pound Pomeranian. I thought that might ease the conversation as most people enjoy little dogs. Our dog was very calm and well-behaved, and remained in my arms.

It took a moment or two for this lady, Marie, to notice that I had something furry in my arms. I asked her if she liked little dogs. All she could do was "mumble." Before I knew it I was bending over and placing the dog next to her in her bed. Immediately this woman came alive!

As I think about it now, it was risky, but worth the risk.

A few minutes later I lifted the dog away and just continued to try and make a one-way conversation with her. She began to smile and I knew I was on safe territory.

Not long after that I told her that I would stop in again next week. She continued to "mumble incoherently." But somehow, I understood that my presence was accepted. After about 20 minutes I felt it was time for me to leave.

All the while I was there, I was thinking to myself, whom do I know that would be just the "right person" to befriend this lady on a regular basis and become a part of her life.

I never referred her to the ministry. *She* was to become *"my new friend."* When I phoned the man who called me about this woman's need, I told him that the Lord had located someone to visit this lady ... *me*.

In the following weeks, I was learning how to have a complete conversation with her, even without her saying a word. I remember thinking that I'll just talk with her as though she understands me. It was the beginning of summer, and each time I visited, she would either be in bed or would be sitting in her wheelchair watching television.

One day I took her blanket off the bed, wrapped it around her legs and off we went ... "outside." I would take her around the neighborhood in her wheelchair. She seemed to just "glow" during this outing.

On one such visit, I took our little dog with us on our neighborhood tour and placed her in Marie's lap, and off we went down the street. Then the "miracle" happened. I heard her beginning to speak. I could hardly believe my ears. No, she wasn't speaking to me, she was speaking to our little dog as she gently held and petted it during the entire outing.

Each week her words became more understandable. Once she began to speak, she never stopped. She never went back to mumbling.

This relationship went on for about 3 years. Each week I would come with goodies to eat, or bring my little dog for special cuddles and walks in the neighborhood.

I remember one time when I went to visit "Miss Marie" she was in the social room. Everyone was sitting around playing a word game. I entered the room with our little Pomeranian, Abby. Miss Marie perked up immediately and held out her hands to hold our little dog. What I didn't expect was that ten other people in the circle wanted to hold this furry friend as well. The visit was longer this week, but it was worth every furry moment.

The Lord was about to move us to a northern state. I missed Marie so very much. Within that year, I believe, she was moved back to where the original couple would be closer for regular visits.

My own parents lived some 2200 miles away, and I had always wondered who would be there to help them when they needed help in their senior years. I lived so far away from them, and I just couldn't grasp why the Lord was allowing me to befriend Marie at a time when I was so concerned about how my own parents would be being cared for.

To my surprise, the Lord arranged that for me about 10 months later. I was privileged to care for my dad, and later have my mom live in my home full-time for almost three years.

Miss Marie was a treasure to me. She taught me in a very quiet way, how a smile, a hug, and an occasional quick visit can change the course of a person's day. One day, I'll get to have a wonderful reunion with her in heaven.

Someone asked me one time, how can you enter a Care facility and make a difference. My response is always the same:

> *It's not about you. It's about genuinely loving others – even with a smile and a little pat on the arm; and allowing the Lord to take it from there. These visits also change your attitude and your heart.*

*Just walking into a person's room at these facilities and interacting with someone through a wave and a smile can make all the difference in the world – **their world and yours!***

Help for a Friend ... for Such a Time as This

We were moving again – this time from the hot, arid climate of Arizona to British Columbia with its lush green environment and abundance of "liquid sunshine." We had not lived in Canada for a number of years, but God directed us to return to the lovely corner of B.C.

We were attending a church and reconnecting with a number of people we met there some years before. One particular Sunday morning it was announced that a man in our congregation had suffered a critical heart attack.

The couple was well known in the church and had developed many friendships over the years, and together with many others we prayed for this man and his dear wife.

Our friend had required quadruple by-pass surgery and made it through. He was now in the long process of recovery. My husband and I heard that many people were visiting him regularly now that he was home from the hospital, but we wanted to be sensitive to his need of rest and recovery.

Several weeks passed, and his wife was writing beautiful emails documenting his progress so that the large circle of friends were kept up-to-date on his condition.

Of course, people reach out in love, but they can often forget that someone who is convalescing needs a lot rest; not to mention, the care-givers as well. This couple was socially vibrant and they loved to have people around, and trying to restrict visitors was not easy. Though these visits were wonderful when they were physically able, a steady flow of visitors was becoming overwhelming.

About six weeks later his wife quietly appeared at church on a Sunday. Since this couple would often sit in the same general area as us each week, we were delighted to have a brief moment with her after the service. We mentioned that we had avoided coming over for a visit as we wanted to be sensitive to their need of rest.

She smiled and said, "Come on over now." We fumbled around trying to respond, but her invitation was so compelling, we agreed, though we would only stay 30 minutes, no more.

As we entered their family room, we saw her husband resting on the sofa covered up with a nice blanket. We approached, and said we just wanted to say "hello" and let him know we cared about him. He wasn't up to a long visit, but in the thirty or so minutes of being together, we hoped our presence would lift his spirits.

As he spoke about his pain and where he was uncomfortable, my inner antennas received a message. My mind went right into gear, and though I am neither a physician nor a nurse, I do have some experience in relieving tension through neck, back and arm massages. For the moment, I just listened to my friend share his concerns.

My first thought was that I did not know this couple well enough to offer a gentle massage a couple times a week. Though I was almost bursting at my seams to do this, I restrained myself and just kept quiet.

About a week later, I phoned to ask what was included in his diet. I had in mind to make them a meal and bring it over. After she shared a few things, I told her that she should expect a dinner delivery at 5 o'clock that same evening. She laughed and said it wasn't necessary, but I paid no attention to her comment and told her dinner was underway.

In the short journey to their home, I had such joy in this meals-on-wheels expedition. I peeked into the family room to say "hello" to the patient. He seemed delighted to have visitors, but again he commented about his stiffness and inability to relax in a number of places in his upper body. I think I prayed with him and then left them to enjoy some roast chicken and trimmings.

A few days later I phoned to see when I could stop by to collect my plates from the meals-on-wheels dinner. My thought had been to ask for an appropriate time for this task, but I discovered that "soon" was "now!"

On the phone, her tone of voice was filled with stress, sadness, and a real sense of being overwhelmed. I was only too familiar with this emotional state. Her tears were my invitation. I told her I'd be over in a few hours with another dinner and that she was not to refuse my offer.

I knew deeply and instinctively that I was prompted to make that phone call, and I breathed a quick prayer: "Lord, how can I help her? How can I help them both? Lord, show me what is needed."

After the phone conversation, I knew without a shadow of a doubt that the Lord was opening doors of opportunity with this dear couple; however, at this point, I had no idea what the type of opportunity could be that would emerge.

After showing up with something for them to eat later in the day, I realized that this woman needed more than dinner that night. Her husband's health situation, as well as her new responsibilities, weighed heavily on her own heart and physique. She was lovingly endeavoring to do too much. She needed something, and soon.

My arrival could not have been more welcomed. It was a bright sunny day, and she suggested we sit outside for a while where she began to share her heart. During the course of our conversation, I felt free to tell her some of the things I had learned from being a caregiver myself just a few years earlier.

Our conversation was simple since she mostly needed a listening ear, a caring heart and personal encouragement. Of course, she needed physical rest as well, but this would have to be a self-imposed rest.

We talked lovingly about boundaries that she would need to set for their "recovery" so that she and her husband could still enjoy others, but with loving limits.

After our talk I offered to give her a massage with olive oil. This simple little massage left her laying like a soft down pillow on the lounge chair on their patio. Seeing that our conversation was dwindling, I went in to see her husband. He had observed the massage treatment on the back patio area and he wondered if he could have one as well.

Though healing, he still experienced stiffness and ongoing tightness in his shoulder. We positioned him comfortably in a chair with feet up and readied him for a massage. There was not much conversation during the next 45 minutes, except for a series of sounds indicating relief from pain. At the end, I could see that both he and his wife were so relaxed resembling two limp noodles hanging in the lawn chairs.

It had been exciting to be allowed into their home, and hearts; but now, with their specific invitation, I was finally able to do what I had wanted to do weeks ago.

Buoyed with success, I was bursting with enthusiasm and asked them both if this "soothing massage" would be something they would enjoy twice a week for a while? Are you kidding? There was an immediate and enthusiastic response from them both.

Remember, prior to this man's health challenge I had been floundering a bit after our move to this new area. I had asked the

Lord if He would open up some kind of opportunity where I could be used. The visit that day with this couple was my answer.

What a joy and privilege getting to know this couple in a wonderful new and transparent way. I was also grateful to God that I could serve this couple through their difficult journey by allowing me the privilege of serving and loving them in this most meaningful way. The Lord reminded me that we were never meant to walk through trials alone, and this was evident as my heart was woven together with this couple.

Today this couple is doing marvelously, and our friend's heart is right on course ... God's course for His life. I was grateful and privileged to play a small part of God's encouragement and healing in their lives at such a crucial season.

God chooses to use people who will love, care, listen and share with us. We will all walk through difficult or painful seasons, and doing so allows us to bear one-another's burdens, lightening their load. And there's no greater bond on this earth.

Let us keep our eyes and ears open to the pain and challenges faced by others. Who knows how God might want to use us to comfort others in their journey?

A 3 x 5 Birthday Card

Hallmark cards are lovely, but sometimes they just aren't available. It was my first day of work at this new company. I was being given the usual tour, and shown around my work area. After the tour, I was taken to where my desk was located.

Since it takes time to settle into a new job, organizing my desk was my first priority. My new boss was very cooperative and understanding, so I was left on my own for the morning to get the supplies I needed.

It was not long before a boisterous employee made her way over to my area. I was not sure why she needed to come by ... perhaps she just needed to check out the new hire. She seemed to have a habit of lingering around my area of the office that morning. I think one of the secretaries in our department was a friend of hers, so I assumed that may have been the reason for her frequent visits.

As is often the case, the office grapevine provides information about special events. However, today's announcement came from this young lady's gentle but firm announcement that today was her birthday. I didn't pay any attention to her announcement since I was new and I didn't know her. Besides, in observing her personality, I was not drawn toward her enough to just join uninvited to her celebration.

I did sense however a gentle nudge within prompting me that I should take notice of this gal. Of course, at first, I simply dismissed the "nudges." There was no let up. It increased to the point that I found myself searching my desk for anything resembling a birthday greeting.

Being new, I did not have a selection of cards at hand. But oddly, I felt like the Lord was moving me to just grab something cute and write Happy Birthday on it.

Well, the only artsy supplies I could find in my desk was a white 3x5 card and a felt-tipped pen. Next, I began rummaging through my purse and found one stick of chewing gum. That's the extent of a potential birthday gift I could manage on such short notice.

Please note that I'm not the brightest button on the shirt when it comes to "crafts." I wondered what in the world could a person do with these three items. So, I folded over the 3x5 card, lengthwise, and taped the stick of gum inside the folded card. I wrote HAPPY BIRTHDAY on the front side. On the back, I wrote "this is not a Hallmark card," as if that identification was necessary, and voila, a not-so-wonderful birthday card was ready for delivery.

It took me awhile to figure out where her desk was located. I remained alert for the rest of the morning following my simple "artistic card design session was over," waiting to figure out where the delivery would occur. At the end of her next appearance, I followed her from a distance to find out where to make the Hallmark delivery.

When it was my break time, I meandered over to her area looking ever-so-innocent and ready for my delivery. Ah ha, she was away from her desk, so I placed the card on top of her desk and made my exit.

It didn't take long for the card to be discovered. I could hear her coming my way. She was pausing here and there asking others if they put anything on her desk. Apparently, my facial expression let the beans out of the bag. She burst out with "did you give me this card?" Well, I sheepishly nodded. I thought she was going to go into tears. She was overwhelmed that I took the time to do such a sweet thing. About this time, my jaws were parting, as I couldn't believe that she was so touched by such an "insignificant little card."

For the rest of that day, she repeatedly stopped by my desk and thanked me. She was even showing off to others this very simple "handmade card" telling them she received it from me, a brand-new employee.

Well, what does all this tell us? That people love being remembered…even if it's only an insignificant little 3x5 card that tells them you're thinking of them.

The Scripture verse from the Bible, 1 Peter 2:17 "Honor all men" is so significant. It means to take notice of another, and celebrate the fact they were designed by God.

HAPPY BIRTHDAY TO YOU……whenever that may be!

Honesty at the Bank

When my husband and I lived in Florida, I applied for a job at a local bank. The name of the bank isn't important, but what happened one morning needs to be exposed. I worked as the bank manager's secretary.

Prior to starting I was given a full introduction of bank policies and procedures. Since I had never been employed by a bank before, I took these instructions seriously. I also felt this training would be important for my career.

Another important part of my responsibility was to influence and encourage employees to demonstrate good public relations skills with the bank customers.

I was also in charge of opening new accounts; but more importantly, I was the designated liaison with their large and most important customers.

This is where this story gets interesting. Our largest customer received top priority in the bank's services on their behalf. This meant that the secretary for this corporation could have access and enter the bank before and after regular business hours.

I was to handle all their deposits or withdrawals, along with any other banking requirement this company needed.

I was the contact person for this corporation's representatives, and would personally handle all their transactions. Whenever she entered the bank, my heart would race a little as I was handling more money than I knew where to place the decimal point, if you know what I mean.

Months went by, and she and I, along with the president of this corporation, enjoyed many moments of personal interaction while their business transactions were taken care of with little to no stress—that is, on their part.

I was always keenly aware of the importance of accuracy when it came to dollars and cents.

The day came when you can imagine what happened next. I had made a mistake. It was a big one! It was a $10,000 mistake! I remember it happened after banking hours and going to an outside drive-through teller's booth to make the transaction.

As I returned inside, I was glancing over the paperwork and made the shattering discovery that I had made this HUGE error in the deposit. Talk about heart racing. My mind raced through a range of scenarios in response to my error.

I could have laid the blame on the teller, but that wasn't the truth. With knees knocking, I went into the bank manager's office, for the last time I thought. He was not only the manager; he was my boss.

I quietly told him what happened. I admitted the error. I'm sure that my eyes must have pleaded for mercy. After a teary admission, my boss, with somewhat stoic composure, simply said not to worry. He was so kind. In fact, he himself phoned the president of the corporation and told him about the error and the mistake that I had made and my honesty about what I had done.

At that moment, I expected that my position as the point person for this company would be terminated. But that was not to be. Though I had a good rapport with my boss, I didn't think it would cover a $10,000 error.

With a heavy heart and a sinking feeling I soon went home, and needless-to-say, my dinner appetite left town. For that matter

I didn't sleep well that night either, as I knew that the following morning I would be meeting with the president of this corporation.

I also feared that my mistake would be announced to all of the other employees. They were far more experienced in banking than I, and I was so embarrassed. Morning came and off I went to work.

My heart was beating so fast that I thought my blouse would burst open from the excessive pounding. I actually arrived long before the bank opened. I will never forget what happened next. As I approached my work space, I noticed that there was a nicely wrapped gift package on my desk.

I knew that "termination slips" are not usually graced in elegant wrapping paper. I couldn't believe my eyes. Who in the world would be placing a gift on "my" desk, especially after the discovery of my banking slip-up the previous afternoon?

This beautifully wrapped gift was from the president of this corporation, our largest customer. Alongside the gift was a card, thanking me for my honesty. Inside was a large bottle of my favorite cologne. How did this man know? How could anyone but my husband and the Lord know of my favorite cologne?

Later that morning, when the president of the corporation arrived, he just looked at me and smiled. I think I was small enough to crawl back into the box. I just thanked him for his kindness and understanding, and the LARGE dose of mercy and forgiveness.

He said he wanted me to know that he was so pleased that I was honest enough to admit the mistake and not blame it on another.

I can assure you that from that day on, I triple-checked every transaction. And no, it never happened again. What struck me was that often our admissions to wrong allow us the privilege of being forgiven, and aid us in learning to walk in humility. It also gave me a live illustration of "mercy."

Can You Teach Me to Sew?

Some people fear spiders or snakes. Let me tell you of two of my secret fears I have faced again and again. You will likely chuckle when you hear these. My fear was my *sewing machine*.

Yes, I know that sewing machines are just tools which cannot speak, sing or throw tantrums. They are designed to do a wonderful job of joining fabric in a beautiful, elegantly stitched fashion, which when appropriately sewn, can provide something lovely to wear, adorn a window, or beautify your home.

But in order for a sewing machine to be effective and efficient in operation, its operator first has to lift it out of its case, plug it into the electrical outlet, turn on the switch, and then proceed with material at hand.

My challenge was not the lifting, plugging, or turning on. My "fear challenge" was working with the material. I questioned my skill at moving the material through the needle pathway correctly and in accordance to the given instructions for that pattern – whether a straight line or a decorative contour. After many unsuccessful attempts at this, my sewing machine had been in retirement (the closet) for a long long time.

In high school I took a leap of faith and signed up for a "sewing class." Had it not been for the teacher working with me step-by-step and moment-by-moment, I would never have finished the dress. I should also note that I never wore that dress in public…. ever! Where else would a navy-blue dress with a white collar end up–the trash can, of course!

My second fear is that of following "*directions.*" The way my mind works is that if someone says to me, "just read the directions," my brain simply freezes up. Truthfully, my confidence is sorely lacking on both counts.

Before laughing and finger-pointing, let me ask you, "When was the last time you read instructions for anything – be it a bicycle, assembling furniture, or following computer directions?" Need I say more?

Honestly, I'd love to meet some of the people who write these, apparently user-friendly directions. After reading certain instructions, I often ask, "Why don't they just speak plain English?"

Okay, the stage is set, and I must share a dear friend's attitude about learning anything on the computer. She feels the same about computer instructions as I do, and she goes on to say, "I don't have what you'd call a friendship with my computer, but we are at least on speaking terms."

In my case, I wasn't even on speaking terms with my sewing machine!! My friend's husband had purchased a nice new sewing machine for her. As he was bringing the machine into the house, their ten-year-old son noticed the new arrival and blurted out, "Oh dad, don't take that in the house, she'll kill herself with it.

Many years ago, I was in the home of one of three dear friends. The common "thread" (funny that I should use the word) was that each home had *handmade* window coverings which gracefully adorned their windows.

One morning, as I was doing one of my favorite things (sipping tea from a fine china cup), I asked the friend in whose home I was visiting that day about her drapes (or window coverings as I call them). She proceeded to tell me how one would go about making them. Of course, I was keen to take in every instructional detail, but at the end of her "instructional dissertation," the picture and series of instructions that had accumulated in my mind suddenly faded to black. Everything evaporated from my brain.

A few weeks later, another friend invited me to her home for tea. We sat at her kitchen table as she prepared a fragrant tea. There in front of me were some lovely scalloped curtains. I couldn't help but notice how straight they hung, and I even got a glimpse of the stitches—all in perfect alignment like stringed soldiers.

Yes, you can guess how our conversation turned. As my friend served the tea and I complimented her on the lovely fabric and the design of the window covering before me, she immediately responded without any hint of pride, that she had made them. Of course, now I'm thinking, I've got some clever friends in my life, and here was another one possessing this amazing talent.

I shared my "fear challenge" about directions and she was quick to tell me that she didn't use a pattern. What? No pattern? No instructions? I was now more than interested in what she had to say. When she finished sharing "her instructions," I thought to myself, "Hey, I might be willing to try."

After the tea party in her kitchen, I went home, and the first thing I did was pray. Yes, I spoke with the Lord (who is interested in every detail of our lives) and asked that He would send someone along to help me not only interpret a pattern's instruction sheet, but help me learn how to sew a straight stitch.

You're going to love to see how this adventure ends!!!!!!!!!

Within a few weeks, I was in yet another friend's home, … and guess what? Her window coverings jumped right out at me and told me to take notice and ask questions. I eagerly obeyed my inner prompting. My friend graciously explained how she had made them, and how I could make them as well.

With full disclosure, I shared my fears with her, and she encouraged me by telling me that I could learn how to sew if I was willing to learn. She offered to work with me in the process, though at that point I don't think she was fully aware of what that would involve. It would require a great amount of patience and a sense of humor to get me through.

God answered my prayer for help in walking me through the steps of sewing a beautiful window covering with just the "right person."

This friend was so encouraging and more than on-board with wanting to help me. We made arrangements to spend an "entire day" buying fabric, measuring the patio window, introducing me to my sewing machine, and completing the project, a lovely hunter green window covering.

Understanding my fear, her suggestion for making curtains was to buy an inexpensive hunter green flat twin sheet to go with our home's color scheme. Smart choice I thought. After all, if I ruined it, it would only be a few dollars down the tube.

After a lengthy, but fairly simplistic explanation of what we were going to attempt, I was much more enthusiastic about trying.

The trick about sewing a straight stitch was incredible. I imagine most of you already know about using a piece of masking tape, and placing it in the area to the right of the needle as a guide. Then all I had to do was place the edge of the material along the tape, and voila! A straight stitch.

This friend was a "gift" to me from the Lord. She had made care arrangements for her four children so she could spend those 8 hours with me. We finished the valence, they were gorgeous, and I was very grateful. I called them "poofs" at the time.

That was over 20 years ago, and my sewing has gone from a simple valance, to long and fabric-lined drapes. I've even shown others how to make some elegant window coverings without using a pattern. For some, reading and interpreting instructions can seem easy, for others, it is not. And I am definitely in the "not category."

What I learned from that friend about sewing and creativity with fabric really isn't as important as the principles and people behind it all. Firstly, God! He is the One who helped me deal with my two practical fears. He then directed my steps to a dear person who made herself available to Him to use in another person's life.

There are three words that speak about a person's value: "**ordinary**," "**available**" and "**sacrificial**." Sewing is an **ordinary** activity! My friend's availability to assist me was crucial. She was sensitive to God, and understood that she needed to teach one of God's children how to sew. She also **sacrificed** precious family time for me.

God loves to use both these concepts in our lives. If we make ourselves **available** to whatever God has in store for us in our **ordinary** life, He will bring others into our life's path and bless "them" through us.

My friend, you know who you are. Thank you for being "my teacher and mentor" in this practical area, and now every time I look at a beautiful drapery fabric, a beautiful window treatment, or a twin flat sheet, I give thanks to the Lord for using *you* in my life in such a dear and practical way.

My prayer is that God would "help me see" the **ordinary** opportunities around me, and that I would be **available** to be used, and may I do so **sacrificially** – especially when it's not convenient.

The three words again are: **ORDINARY–AVAILABLE–SACRIFICIAL**. Lord, may these qualities be woven by You into my character that my life may be a blessing to others. Amen

Always Be Yourself – No One is More Qualified: Even if you are in Rollers

As I begin to tell this "real-life event," I want you to know that there will *not* be a corresponding photo attached. The reason, it's not a pretty sight.

The story begins on a day I washed my hair. This is likely not an issue for most of you, but due to my curly hair, I use rollers, and stay within the confines of my home until my hair dries – about four hours. Then I use a flat curling iron to calm my hair in an effort to look presentable to the general public.

I was *under the influence of rollers* with about thirty of those brushed things in my hair. Two hours passed as the renovation process was underway. These are the ones with the pink picks to hold the uncomfortable brushed hair in place on your head.

Since my husband was heading out to our local hardware store, I thought I'd go along for the ride and bring our little dog with us. The plan was that the dog and I would just sit in the air-conditioned car and wait for him on this very hot day. It appeared that the situation was well in hand, and about twenty minutes later my husband returned. I was looking forward to being home soon.

However, because of the way in which he approached the car, I could tell something was brewing. Instead of the driver's side, he came to me and motioned for me to lower the window. Are you kidding, it was 33 degrees Celsius, and rolling down a window would allow the oppressive heat to enter my cool comfort! Perhaps he missed that memo.

He gestured excitedly for me to follow him into the store, exclaiming there was something in the kitchen department he wanted to show me right away. Umm, Mr. Husband, don't you see what you're asking? Can't you see I'm in rollers! Women do not want to appear in public in that condition.

Unfazed, he insisted that I come with him and without delay. Honestly, I could NOT believe he was asking me to expose myself to the general public in this ghastly sight of rollers. He seemed oblivious to my self-conscious predicament and was so insistent I come. There was no escaping this.

So, what does a wife do in this situation? It was time to let my vanity and pride go down the tube. I grabbed the dog and somewhat anxiously left the car. Keeping my head down, I hoped I could avoid eye contact with other customers. As we approached the entrance, a young gal watched customers enter and exit – preferably with their receipts in hand enabling her to check whether their products had indeed been purchased.

For some unknown reason, after she looked at me, I felt *compelled* to explain my appearance. Without thinking, I told her that at their next staff meeting she could announce that some woman had the *guts* to enter their store in "rollers." She began laughing herself to pieces.

Not wanting to draw a crowd, I quickly sought to catch up with my husband, who had rather intentionally moved several yards ahead of me. A few minutes earlier, he plainly demonstrated why he wanted me to come into the store, but now it seemed he didn't want others to see I was with him. First you want to show me something, and now you want to keep your distance! How inconsiderate!!

To my amazement, no one seemed to even look my way. However, with my head down I don't think I would have noticed if they did get a glance.

Once in the appliance department, I looked at the item for which I was being made to suffer. It was now time for me to leave the store, and with my head hung low, we moved toward the exit ... with my beloved way ahead of me. Of course, the same young gal was still at the door, and she broke into laughter again as I approached. But what came next surprised me.

I said again, "Don't forget the lady with rollers who had courageously entered the store!" After her laughter had subsided, she added, "You just made my day!" I realized that rollers are a reality in life and why be ashamed of them. I responded that we need to "*be real and transparent in life,*" and she heartily agreed.

Another way to phrase this aspect of being transparent ... is "be yourself." I could imagine that each of us, at one time or another, has wished to be like someone else. It might be another's looks, shape, personality, giftedness, and we could go on and on. God's Word reminds me that He IS our Creator ... our individual Creator. God designed each of us to be an "original," not a copy of another. Besides, we really aren't true to ourselves if we're trying to be someone else.

Psalm 139:13,14 says," For You formed my inward parts; You covered me in my mother's womb. I will praise You, for I am fearfully and wonderfully made; marvelous are Your works, and that my soul knows very well. My frame was not hidden from You, when I was made in secret...."

Perhaps someone reading this event might say, "I wouldn't have done that for all the money in the world." Or, "Why in the world would she enter a public place decked out in rollers?"

But even though the pride in my (post-roller) appearance was important, I wanted to look past it and hopefully bring laughter to others, even if at my expense while I waltzed through the store.

After walking out of the hardware store, I was thankful that I had left my pride in the car. I was pleased that I made this gal's day. Both she and I couldn't stop laughing, and I made a new friend that day.

I am also making a NOTE TO SELF, "If husband is going out for an extended period of time, and I am in rollers, I'll respectfully stay home."

Yes, this is a true story and as mentioned before, there are NO photos to prove it. You'll just need to trust me on this one. And furthermore, it can be "fun" to be who you were designed to be.

Making a Difference for One!

Before I share this tender-hearted story, I thought it best to introduce "pictorially" the tiny sweetie I'm writing about. Yes, it's a true story of my all-season friend. I've named her Anna. It's a most appropriate name because she is an Anna's Hummingbird.

Anna and I started becoming acquainted about two years ago after we had moved to Surrey, British Columbia – not far from the US border. It did not take long for us to notice the number of hummingbirds in the area.

While moving in, one of the first boxes I unpacked was my yard box which contained my hummingbird feeder. I prepared the necessary recipe (1 part sugar and 4 parts water .. in case you need to prepare a similar buffet for hummingbirds in your area), and located the feeder in just the right spot in our little yard.

This must have been right on their flight-path as this Anna's hummingbird found a brand-new source of nutrition for herself. I made sure that in the warmer months, the feeder was cleaned and refilled with fresh nectar each week.

It was late spring when this inviting food was placed in our yard. My husband and I would enjoy a cup of tea or a latte early in the morning sunshine on the patio. It wasn't long before we would notice a visitor. She announced her arrival with a hummingbird's wee beeping chirps. Just for the fun, I responded with similar sounds. My imitation sounds weren't the best, but this little hummer (as I called her), would respond and beep her chirps back to me. My husband and I laughed and adored her acrobatic presence as she partook of her morning "sweets."

I would find myself throughout the day looking out to see if she was near the feeder. Near the feeder?!! Are you kidding? She was perched comfortably next door in a ten-foot tree overlooking her new "in and out" diner.

In the warm summer months, I would often sit outdoors, and enjoy a cup of tea or an iced tea. I would observe this little bird eating about ten times in an hour out of the feeder. I couldn't believe the volume of liquid such a tiny bird could consume. She is about 1 ½" long and simply adorable.

This feeding frenzy went on for most of the summer and into the fall. After that, I assumed she would fly southward like most other birds. However, as October came around, I noticed she was still perched at the feeder regularly so I kept cleaning and refilling it, thinking that soon she would be heading south for the winter.

I was wrong! As I discovered, not all hummingbirds fly south for the winter. She was going to stay put in our neighborhood. Things were going along as normal until the temperatures began to drop. I phoned the Hummingbird Society in Arizona and checked the internet to see how I could provide a winter diet for this beautiful fine-feathered friend.

Now before I continue you must promise me that you won't turn me in to the "men in the white coats" ... because they know about me already, and are not interested. You see, I'm simply beyond their help.

I was instructed to make sure that the contents of the feeder did not freeze. This moved me to my next purchase which was another hummingbird feeder. Yes, now I have two. One is to be placed out early in the morning, after the sun comes up. The other feeder remains inside (where it can be room temperature). If it's really cold and the contents of the outside feeder are beginning to form ice, I swap it with the other feeder.

An idea came to me via the internet to aid keeping the feeder warmer. I had a pair of fuzzy socks. I took the socks and cut off the toe part and then placed both socks over the first feeder I put outside in the morning. This discovery proved to be a wonderful solution. Even at 25 degrees (-4 Celsius) during the daytime, the feeder would not freeze.

To be honest, I wondered if this bird would be nervous about a feeder being gift-wrapped in socks. The following morning, I placed the "new little diner" on the hook. No problem ... she got stuck right into the food. There was nothing wrong with her appetite.

Perhaps I had been inside too long during winter, but I had another idea. On the wrought iron fencing around our raised patio, I placed Christmas lights – the real tiny ones, and moved the feeder to just outside our back door. This little gal LOVES HER BUFFET selection, so I knew she wouldn't be bothered that I moved it a little closer so we could see her in action more clearly.

It also was hung in a safe environment away from any predators and shown beautifully in the winter sunshine.

What I haven't disclosed is that I was secretly wondering if she would enjoy the Christmas lights ... not to view, but to sit around and be warmed by the lights.

One day I kept looking out to see where in the world she had disappeared to. There were two feeders for her in the yard, one by the fence about 30 feet from our back door, and the other just 1 ½ feet from the door. I kept looking at both feeders but she was nowhere to be found.

As my eyes jumped from one feeder to the other, I neglected to see the obvious. She was now perched ON TOP OF A CHRISTMAS LIGHT! Yes, you're reading correctly. Then she moved to arrange herself in the middle of about six lights. This was keeping her warm. She simply had to lift herself away from the lights and fly only a foot-and-a-half to her feeder and back again.

With close observation, I've found her daily routine to be quite repetitive.

- Arrival at her tree perch between 7:45–8:00 a.m.
- Glance over to see the Christmas lights in the "on" position
- She fluffs her feathers and continues glancing at the buffet chef (that's me–located inside)
- When the chef notices her arrival, she comes outside with the cuisine container, topped off with warm socks
- Chef returns to place the second feeder by the fence (this feeder is right across from "Anna's" tree limb)
- As the chef leaves the feeders, she calls out "Anna" and makes wee hissing sounds to notify Anna that breakfast is now served in the main dining areas
- Anna responds back to the chef with her wee sounds...as if to say "thank you"
- Chef enters the house to go undercover for the day

- About 10 minutes later, Anna flies over for several sips of delight
- About 9:00 a.m. Anna decides to perch on a "Christmas light" which keeps her warm. Sometimes she tires of that one location and then moves to the center of about 6 lights where she's very toasty for the day. Sometimes she adds a little exercise to her routine and swings on the light cord that dangles in mid-air
- At 4:25 p.m. she exits her Christmas light, heads for the closest feeder and drinks for about a full minute to stock up for the night to go into her torpor or sleepy state.

Then ... she takes off for the entire night in a local tree and goes into torpor state where the body reduces to a very low temperature. Thus, the nourishment that she's had all day, and especially at the 4:25 feeding, provides enough warmth for the tree trip and to cuddle down for the night. This same routine is repeated every morning.

This blow-by-blow detail of this little bird not only shows God's incredible design of this little bird – including giving her the ability to reduce her body temperature so low, and then to recuperate and come back to life alive and alert the following morning.

How great is the majesty of God, the Creator of all things Who goes to this kind of extreme detail to care for even these little ones, and in so doing, displays His creative touch not only in our world, but in our lives as well.

I am overwhelmed to think that since He cares so much for a bird that weighs about the same as a nickel, how much more does He care for us? This bird does not worry about life – it just knows that it will be cared for. What would happen if we simply and completely abandon ourselves to Him, and watch Him provide for us ... usually miraculously?

This isn't the end of the story, but the beginning of realizing that little things we can do can make a "great impact" on others, regardless of their size, nationality, color or design.

As God meets our daily needs, let us, in turn, meet the needs of others. This little feathered friend has brought to "light" that I can't help or make a difference in the life of everyone, but ... I CAN MAKE A DIFFERENCE TO ONE! Though we can neither help everyone, nor touch the life of thousands, we can none-the-less be used by Him in meaningful and personal ways to make a difference in the life of another. What is our part in this formula? Like the little bird, we simply trust Him to meet us and others at our point of need.

Each day, let's ask God to help us be alert to the "one" that He would have us encourage, help, show a kindness to, or listen to. You never know, we CAN MAKE A DIFFERENCE in our world.

I couldn't help but show two more photos of little Anna. Look close under her tummy, and you'll see a tiny Christmas light.

The Christmas light is right under her lower tummy just above her tail!

Learning to Push & Pull

You know, in life we never stop learning. But having to learn new things can be intimidating to me. I should note that I had recently moved to Australia, and there was a lot of learning to do.

Of course, we learn from books, teachers, parents, friends, Google, and a myriad of other sources. Though not all of these are accurate or worth spending a lot of time and energy, there are occasions that do squeeze us into the "now it's time to learn how to ____," and you can fill in the blank.

One morning while returning from a meeting I saw the gas indicator light blink on to "E". Thankfully I saw a service station ahead of me. My first thought was to wait a few days until my husband was home and let him fill the tank.

In all honesty, my reason for hesitating was that I didn't know "how to do this task," and felt uncomfortable attempting it on my own. It may sound foolish, but in moving to a new country there were literally dozens and dozens of new "changes and challenges" that God was helping me overcome, and I wasn't up to how to "pump gas" into the tank.

I now had an opportunity of moving out of my "comfort zone" – where I most enjoy living – and face an "inner fear" of such a mundane task. God wants to help us face all our fears, large or small, huge or insignificant, with His strength and help.

As I came within a block of the service station, I made the decision to pull into the area and asked the Lord to help me, in whatever way He chose in this "new adventure."

You know we can say, "Well, I trust the Lord," but it wasn't until I pulled into the service station and got out of the car did, I show by my actions that I was actively going to trust Him. He wants to meet "all our needs," not just some of them ... and believe me, living close to "empty" on my gas gauge was an immediate need.

It was time for the "learning how to fill your car's gas tank in Australia" class, and I needed to pay attention. The car was dangerously close to empty, and so it made sense for me to not just register for the class, but pass the practical.

Those of you who have moved to a different country with the many varied cultural and practical ways of doing life understand the STRESSES. For starters gasoline is called petrol in Australia. Not too bad. That's a good start. My husband usually handles that task, while I enjoy the scenery from the passenger seat. In all honesty, I've been spoiled.

Since my husband was out of the country this weekend, and the gas tank was demanding attention, the task was mine and mine alone.

In my defense, I should add that I had not been shown "how" to fuel up in Australia. It was simple from where I used to live, but here, I had no idea what to do. I had been under the assumption that all gas stations were similar, but ... trust me, not all service stations around the world are the same.

Had the following sequence of events been recorded on You Tube, there would easily have been several hundred-thousand hits by now. I approached the station slowly and cautiously. Before arriving at the pump, I needed to locate which side of the car the opening was to refill the tank. I'd like to speak to the manufacturer on this one, because there were no pictures on the dash showing me where the filling spout was located.

On pulling up to the appropriate gas pump, I asked the Lord for help. Goodness knows, He knew I needed it! My eyes were busy searching out for the first person in sight. Yes, I found one and she was just completing her fill up and looked available. I introduced my first need. I wanted to know where to place my credit card to pay for my upcoming purchase. She was smiling from ear to ear, and I'm not certain if that was her normal demeanor, or she was about to burst into laughter at the ignorance being displayed before her. We both had a laugh though, and that helped me relax.

She was very astute and quickly advised me of my options. I could grab that hose with the enlarged handle and fill the car at that point and pay afterwards; or, I could take my card inside the station and pay there. So, without delay, I pranced into the building, my confidence building. It is unfortunate that my cell phone camera was not able to capture the attendant's face as he watched my approach to his counter. He had an odd smile (at least I interpreted it as a smile). I didn't expect a lengthy conversation; so, I handed him my card and said that I wanted to fill up the car and then come back in to pay the amount.

Then the unanticipated dialogue began. "What part of the United States are you from?" I knew better than to say, "How did you know I was from America?" It's obvious for Australians to detect your accent. My brief question gave away my cultural roots. After the "interview" with the clerk, he told me what to do. Now, with that under my belt, I went back out to the car. At first, I couldn't open the little door that held the opening to the tank. Another obvious detail I hadn't asked my husband about.

After studying the dash board of my vehicle and perusing all the buttons, I located a picture that looked like a release button for the fuel tank.

Looking through the Lens of . . .

Time didn't permit me to look around to see if anyone was observing this display of "automotive ignorance" by this woman trying her best to just simply fill up her car. I was focused now and on a mission. How difficult could it be? I had all my instructions memorized. I opened the tank door, turned to the pump, pulled it towards the gas opening and then another obstacle arose. Where in the world is the latch that you pull or push to get the gas flowing?

Breathing deeply now, I began asking the pump handle (under my breath of course) where in the world do I make it work as there was no latch to press or pull. By now my confidence was about as absent as the fuel from the pump. It was apparent that I needed to meet another "new friend" at the pump area of the service station for further directions. I verbally grabbed the first person I saw and shared my dilemma.

It's amazing how helpful people can be when you're in a "pickle at the pump." Her instructions were clear as a bell. "Just press the button!" This is simple and quite obvious ... if you know where the button is.

A quick visual inspection of the handle revealed .... Nothing!! By now this woman had the same "ear-to-ear smile" the last gal had; and I doubt it was her personality oozing out. She was exercising restraint from bursting out in hysterical laughter. The facts, plain and simple were, she couldn't believe I didn't see the "obvious."

The button that everyone was referring to was HUGE, and right on top. As I'm asking, "Is this the one?" "Yes, she responded. Just PULL the spout out and PUSH the button." The petrol came guzzling out into the car tank. I was thrilled, to say the least. I stood there proud as a peacock that the gas was flowing effortlessly into my car at lightning speed.

Now it was time to reconnect with my third "new friend" inside the station at the cash register. I must admit I was so pleased there were no other customers in the store. The attendant processed the card, and just looked at me with a big smile. "See you again!" I couldn't exit the store fast enough.

When I pulled away, I thought to myself, "Well, I've just shown my ignorance to three new friends, and all three were smiles through the process. I also assumed that all three people would be sharing their laughable episodes observing me at the gas station at their dinner table that night. But it didn't matter to me, because this learning curve brought smiles to three strangers and helped me realize that God would provide my "every need." Who knows, I may see them again at another "gas-filling event."

What "needs" are you currently facing that God would like to be a part of?

Delights in the Double Semi

At first, this story may seem unbelievable, but it's true nonetheless. One summer my husband and I were in New Zealand visiting his parents. While there, we would use their small, but comfortable Ford Anglia car, which by the way, is not designed for anyone over six feet.

One particularly warm afternoon while driving, we were enjoying the car's natural budget air-conditioning ... all the windows rolled down. It not only seemed as if we were the only ones on the road – we were – it was that lonely. Unconcerned about traffic, we enjoyed touring the countryside that afternoon.

The solitude and serenity of the country was suddenly interrupted by some rather rude noises from the car. It was sputtering as if we were running out of gas. A quick glance at the gauges showed more than enough fuel to take us home.

My husband eased over to the side of the road and began the trial-and-error approach to determine the cause. I must admit, my husband is amazing at most things mechanical ... as long as he has access to YouTube. At that time however, we neither had access to the internet nor a smart phone. GPS was unheard of – as least for civilian use.

Besides, I am sure the GPS voice would have said in its helpful, neutral tone, "Turn around. The next available service station is 20 kilometers away!" We didn't need a voice telling us the obvious: we were far from everything, on a lonely road, and mechanically something was so very wrong with the car.

I can't remember exactly what he extracted from the car. Could it have been like going to a dentist to remove an offending tooth? Whatever it was, he removed it from the front end of the car, and before he began walking, he left us with these instructions to the three soon-to-be-alone passengers to stay put. He would simply find a ride, and go to the next town and have the part repaired. With no idea of how far that town would be, we sat like mute, doe-eyed orphans in the car – quiet but hopeful.

With my father and mother-in-law in the back seat, and me in the front, we sat in a fog of silence as no one had any ideas of how to solve our automotive-dilemma. After a while, we began discussing our helpless state, and I was reminded of the scripture passage that says that when you're in trouble and belong to the Lord, call on Him, and He is a very present help in trouble. An idea struck me: dad, the professional musician in the back seat, just "happened" to have his clarinet with him.

The more we thought about this, the more determined we were about sharing our cares with the Lord. Together with that sharing, we should also sing some praise choruses, since our own professional musician could accompany us.

For a while our tiny little car became our church and concert hall as we told the Lord about our need for a car repair, and the provision of just the right part for the car wherever my husband had been driven to. Then, we began to sing. We must have sung five or six choruses from our reasonably vast choral repertoire. More than an hour passed by, and there was no sign of my beloved fix-it man.

Our energetic singing, together with the rising temperature in this remote part of the country, made us quite warm. We explored our memories for more choruses, and continued to sing, reminding ourselves that God knew our exact location and predicament. We followed the Bible's instruction of being encouraged in the Lord. We were doing that, with all our heart and lungs.

In the quietness of the New Zealand countryside, I am sure distant grazing sheep were blessed with the many praise choruses and music that issued through the open car windows. During this time, not one vehicle went past us.

Then it happened. A HUGE truck approached in the distance, and began to slow down. It was a double (I did say double) semi-truck! You don't see them very often and we were astonished at its size and length.

If anything, it would at least stir up some air as it passed by our car. What took our breath away is that the driver actually stopped this rig and pulled to the side of the road.

He asked about our situation, and we responded with "We don't know what's wrong, but we hoped that someone would soon be returning with the needed part."

After understanding the situation, the driver knew there was really nothing he could do for us. We, on the other hand, certainly sure appreciated his care by stopping.

He then said he had a treat for us, and asked our somewhat warm, doe-eyed group if "... we liked ice cream?" I quickly thought, "Does a rabbit like carrots?" We couldn't get a YES out fast enough.

He went to the rear of his semi and opened the doors. Inside the trailer was a truck load of ICE CREAM, and all the flavors you could think of. He then asked, "Name your favorite flavor?"

He pulled out a pint of our "requested favorites" and handed one to each of us – with spoons too. Did we rejoice and give thanks to the Lord, or what!!!!

We were thrilled out of our socks, and the truck driver was so pleased to have helped us. Due to the heat, and while gobbling down our ice cream, a thought came to me. My husband would never believe this double semi-truck full of ice cream story. The only way he would believe is if he could SEE & TASTE the evidence.

Before the ice cream man, I mean the truck driver, could close the semi doors, I asked if he had any Rocky Road in his ice cream inventory. HE DID, and he gave me a pint of it. I quickly wrapped the package in newspaper and placed it in the cooler in our over-heated car and, hoping it would hold together until my husband returned.

The semi hadn't been gone more than ten minutes when the auto fix-it man arrived. We had just finished our pint of ice cream, so all the evidence of the Lord's help was consumed, but thanks to the cooler, my husband was about to hear the story of his life.

The repair only took him a couple minutes and we were all standing around, anxiously awaiting the opportunity to share our "show and tell" event. With no time to waste, I told my husband the story. You can guess his reaction—No, he'd never heard of such a thing, and didn't believe me about the big ice cream truck.

Well, the proof is in the pudding, or shall I say, the ice cream, and I hurried to the cooler before the "show part" disappeared into goo.

We handed him a spoon and I reached into the cooler, pulled out and unwrapped the pint of (his favorite) Rocky Road ice-cream. His eyes were like golf balls and once he began eating, he was a true believer. This was all provided by the Lord because we prayed, and thanked God for His provision … even before it happened.

To date, I've never seen another double-semi truck filled with ice cream. Now, whenever I hear the white tiny ice cream truck playing its jingle in our neighborhood, my thoughts and heart goes back to the semi-truck loaded with frozen desserts. I just smile with delight at God's goodness and sweetness to us that day.

Overnight on a Boat

Have you ever been invited to join friends for a lovely late afternoon dinner on an island? Up to this point, my response would have been no. Not many of our friends have a boat. Though I am sure many have little boats – those used in a tub while soaking.

We had some dear friends who wanted us to join them "on the water" and our destination was to be Orcas Island in Washington State. That island paradise is host to a beautiful restaurant and hotel. This was our planned destination.

We were thrilled to be invited and join them in this adventure. Arrangements were made, and a time all set up to meet them at a particular marina. Keep the word "adventure" in mind through the rest of this story.

To be honest, I'm not exactly thrilled about boats, and even less enthusiastic about being over water. I don't mind the bathtub or water less than three feet deep. My husband assured me this water adventure would prove to be a delightful two-and-a-half-hour pleasure trip to this beautifully landscaped island.

As my husband waxed eloquently about the safety features of this 26-foot Bayliner, he assured me that our friend, the captain, was trustworthy, competent, and experienced. He had owned and operated many boats in his life, and the scenic trip in itself would be a thrilling experience, not to mention a delightful early dinner.

What could go wrong??? Somehow my mind immediately went into defensive mode, and all I could think about was: are there sufficient life jackets, what was the depth of the water in route, and how long this "cruise" would take.

The long-awaited day arrived and we happily boarded their beautiful boat. The man's wife gave us a grand tour ... which lasted about two minutes. I mean how long does it take to locate everything on a 26' boat? My only concern was the "ladies' room" (or head ... in nautical lingo). It wasn't large, but sufficient to meet the needs of all on board.

At this point, I was very relaxed and enjoying their company, their friendship, and the comforts of this pleasure craft. Bear in mind, we haven't left the dock yet, but we are on the water.

I also recall, and not that vaguely, our friend assuring us that he had checked the gas gauge and everything was in order, and that his boat had a *full* tank of fuel! This small detail is important to remember.

We pulled away from the dock and into the waters. After cruising along on a lovely sunny afternoon, we noticed the island and could now see the restaurant off in the distance. My mind relaxed, thinking, "This is great! I can be OFF THIS BOAT in twenty minutes and on LAND!!"

In every story, there should be some drama. Let me introduce you to some now. Do you recognize the sounds an engine makes when it has an "empty" fuel tank? It's like a sputter, oozing of air, and then nothing. The calm of the afternoon and the noise of the engine was suddenly overtaken by silence. We all wondered what happened. After all, he had a full tank of gas, and the route he took us on would not have used half that amount.

After a few "umms" and "awes," he announced that the fuel tank was apparently .... *empty!*

My usual calm demeanor is not prone to panic attacks, but I was certainly willing to exercise one right there and then. I remember

Looking through the Lens of . . .

my eyes enlarging like dinner plates, and my heart beginning to race. Our competent captain calmly reassured us all would be well. As much as I liked this guy, my faith in his ability went out the window, or more appropriately, "overboard" at that moment!

Mentally, my defensive mode kicked in as I thought of our immediate circumstance: Powerless and adrift in over 600 feet deep water and with not another boat in sight. You know how a voice travels smoothly over water don't you? Well, even a scream wouldn't have helped at this point.

Of course, this is the ideal time to call on the Lord! I grabbed his wife's arm, and we both prayed. In case He was not aware, we informed the Lord of our location, gave details of our delay, the depth of the water, and the fact we were alone with no one in sight to help us. I could hardly get an amen out fast enough.

I recalled the scripture that God will meet our every need. There was no doubt, WE WERE IN NEED. There was nothing we could do but "be still ... and wait." Not forgetting what we had asked God, I kept rehearsing my little prayer to keep me focused. We never know when or how God is going to answer our prayers, but He always responds in the best way and for His glory.

Believe me there would be no taking personal credit for any positive result in this scenario.

About 25 minutes later, the grandest thing happened. Another boat came into view ... almost out of nowhere it seemed. I know it didn't drop from the sky, but it appeared and our hearts began to pump again. We yelled out for help and it began heading our way.

After determining what could be done, the other boat extended a rope and towed us into the harbor where we arrived 20 minutes later. We just rejoiced! His wife and I shared how we had talked to the Lord and asked for Him to send help. And HE DID!

We exited the boat, and went to the restaurant for a very late dinner. By the time we got back to where the boat was moored it was too late to obtain fuel. I can't explain that, but the facts were that it was too late to purchase fuel. We would now need to spend the night "on this floating hotel."

This was all new to me ... and here I am about to experience a real night on a boat. I'm not a fan of cruises, and I have never been on one, and so you know where I'm coming from.

Accommodations for sleeping were great. We each went to our little bedroom facility and cuddled in for the night. Then it began ... the gentle lapping of the small waves alongside the boat. I couldn't sleep since it was like sleeping next to a grandfather clock. In that in-between state of sleep and wakefulness, you hear every tick of the clock, and then are reminded by chimes every quarter hour, half hour and hour.

Somewhere between four and five in the morning I fell asleep, only to be woken early so we could purchase some fuel. I was so weary that I think they could have pulled me along on a tugboat and I would have slept right through the event, noise and all.

Now there are three morals in the story. First, make sure your fuel gauge works properly, and accurately reflects the amount of fuel it contains. Second, triple check your tank to make sure it is, in fact, full, and third, and most importantly, always remember that if you belong to the Lord, He is the One to "call on and look to" for help.

A Word of Encouragement

Our words "to others" and "about others" are so important. I'd venture to say they are life changing! Proverbs 18:21 says, "Death and life are in the power of the tongue."

This story occurred many years ago when I was a junior in high school. Summer break had ended and my second-last year of high school was about to commence.

I already had one year of Spanish and thought I could attempt another year. That was a wrong choice. The teacher soon appeared after the students were seated and began waxing eloquent in Spanish, and I was trapped in a second-year Spanish class.

Since we had all taken first year Spanish, this man assumed that we all had made straight A's, and could now communicate fluently in his native tongue.

Unfortunately, it took me almost six weeks before I had the courage to admit that I barely understood a word said in his class.

It wasn't rocket science for me to finally admit I needed to abandon this language tuition, and embark on another course of study. There was shorthand! In thinking ahead for my future employment, I assumed that being able to learn this skill could prove to be a real plus in the secretarial field.

I tried graciously to admit that language wasn't my forte and so I signed up for a shorthand class with Miss May. When I entered her class, she was very receptive which immediately endeared me to her.

The challenge—I was now six weeks behind all the other shorthand students.

This "kind and patient" teacher agreed to stay after class each day to try and bring me up-to-speed (and I mean that literally) on the basics of Gregg shorthand.

Amazingly, after about six weeks of this after-school study and instruction time, I was now in sync with the other students. I'm not saying I was the brightest by a long shot, but at least I was now participating in the same chapter of the book as the rest of the class.

Miss May would take us on field trips and fun events. I recall that our class even spent an evening in her apartment making taffy. She was a teacher who became a friend and a mentor all in one.

No wonder everyone enjoyed her class and her approach to teaching. She made learning "fun." The days flew by, and my first year of shorthand was over. That deserves recognition right off the bat, doesn't it?

Soon, another summer break was over and it was back-to-school for my senior year. Miss May had married during that summer, and we now addressed this beautiful woman by her married name.

Perhaps because I had so enjoyed this class, I decided to enlist for a second year of shorthand. As we entered her class, I sat at the far wall, second row. Funny the things we remember!

This woman not only taught shorthand, she taught good posture as well. I know that, because so often she would meander by my desk, requesting me to sit up straight and pull my shoulders back. She still comes to mind when I'm attentive to my posture.

You know, no one ever corrected my posture before, but I discovered you sure appear more confident in appearance if you're sitting up straight, not to mention the appreciation of your vertebrae.

I wanted to write about this dear person, because she was the first person that I can remember in my life who ever gave me a WORD OF ENCOURAGEMENT.

I can't recall all the details of our work assignment in class, but we were asked one day to write a business letter, using the right punctuation, salutation, complimentary closing, date, etc. You know, a real official-like letter. Every student submitted their letters in class on the specified day.

She must have been very busy that night, because the following day she came to class with our "letter-writing efforts" in hand complemented by her assigned grades in the upper right-hand corner.

If my memory serves me right, she used a "red" marking pen, so that her comments and grade evaluation were displayed boldly.

I think (?) I got an A. Her comments that appeared at the top of my assignment and her words are forever etched in my mind and in my heart: "Dianne, you have a flair for letter-writing!"

That sentence changed my life!!! Can you believe it? You see, I had been raised without any verbal encouragement, and I often felt as though I would never amount to much.

This phrase, written at the top of my typed business letter, was proof that this teacher could see "potential" in me.

Towards the end of the year, the business faculty was going to present awards. One award to be given was entitled the most "Outstanding Achievement Award."

We gathered for this event in the school gym. I remember purposely sitting at the top section of the bleachers as I confidently knew that my name would not be heard echoing through the PA system in the auditorium. I was comfortable and ready to enthusiastically applaud whoever was chosen.

I did notice that one of my classmates from the shorthand class had positioned herself on the bottom row of bleachers, providing easy access to receive an award if her name was called.

She was a very bright student and received straight A's if I remember correctly. My assumption was that she had assumed that she would be chosen, and so positioned herself in that convenient location.

Several awards were presented, and then the moment came to announce the name for the achievement award. MY NAME was announced! I could hardly believe it.

I think friends seated around me had to confirm it to me, and move me out of my comfortable position at the top of the auditorium so I could get down the twenty or more rows to receive the award.

I was given the award and $100. I'm still amazed. But let me share what was more meaningful than the plaque and the $100.

It was the fact that this teacher believed in me, and that she felt that *"my life had potential."* How was I to know that she thought my life had any potential in the business sphere if she hadn't told me in writing on my first attempt at composing a business letter?

This isn't the end of the story. We became friends after I got out of high school, and we have remained friends to this day. I will always "cherish her" as an encourager personified! Why? Because she took the time to let me know that my efforts and skills were beginning to blossom, and that I had potential.

I'm not the best with writing or authorship, but what's really important is that she affirmed me in an area in which God was working and preparing me.

Proverbs 18:21; 16:21 have something to say about this: "Death and life are in the power of the tongue." "The wise in heart will be called prudent, and sweetness of the lips increases learning."

Who in your life needs YOUR WORD OF ENCOURAGEMENT?

Let's all keep a perceptive eye on the potential in others ... and then, be sure and communicate that to them.

Our words can serve as a CONSTRUCTION ZONE or a DEMOLITION SITE!

On the Loose at Night

Early morning is my best time, so I'm in bed by 9:30 or 10:00 p.m. Sometimes, if I want to relax before bedtime, I get adorned in my pajamas. There's no need for a description, but be assured, they're comfortable.

My husband was out of town at the time, so it really didn't matter what time I engaged the "sleepy time" position. I was very tired that evening, and I couldn't wait to lay my head on the pillow. There would not be any need for counting sheep.

In the stillness of the night, I heard some odd noises. At first, I tried to ignore them, after all it was late and I was tired. I suddenly remembered my husband wasn't there to check out the sounds, and this caused me to get out of bed and look out the window.

It didn't take long to determine the source of the noise. It was a neighbor around the corner calling her dog. No problem, I thought. If I could hear her, surely her dog would hear and respond accordingly.

Please understand that I love animals, but since my neighbor did not stop her appeal to her dog, I wondered if I should head down the stairs and out our front door to see if two voices could coax this canine homeward.

My goodness, I can't go out with my pajamas on, can I? Her pleas and cries seemed to become more insistent; to the point where my pajamas came along with my body, right down the steps and swirling out the front door.

Before I could pause and take the time to really consider what I was doing, I found myself running towards her home. Let me also say that I grabbed my robe to keep me warm and covered for this pursuit down the street.

The woman was almost in tears when I arrived just 60 seconds after leaping out of my warm comfortable bed. "What's wrong," I asked. Her dog had got out of the yard and wouldn't come home. I gathered by this information that he wasn't "street smart" to figure out to where he should return.

Without thinking (who thinks straight after 11 pm anyway), I began not only joining the search, but soon directing the "search and rescue." I suggested she grab her car keys, get her car out of the garage, and we'd drive around the neighborhood together.

She agreed to the suggestion and took off like a startled cat, into the house, and moments later the garage door squeaked open and off we went in her car.

I prayed silently before her foot made contact with the car's accelerator asking for God's help in locating her furry little family friend.

Here's what the scenario actually looked like. As she drove, I began yelling out the dog's name at the top of my lungs. I can't remember what his name was; but suffice it to say it appeared as only one syllable, thank goodness.

Can you imagine if I had to vocalize two syllables in a moving car late at night? I vowed right then and there that if I encountered a neighbor the following day, and they asked if that was my voice they heard calling out the previous evening, I would deny everything.

We drove around and around the blocks in the community. With the movement of the car, I found myself repeating her dog's name about once every 5 seconds. I'm sure we woke up a number of our neighbors who had expected an undisturbed night's sleep. If not, we certainly disrupted their attempt to snooze.

I was rehearsing in my mind, "Yes the Lord cares and knows all about this." He knows I want to help my neighbor. After all, if that was our little dog (who also wasn't street smart) was lost, I'd give anything if someone gave up the comfort of their home and tried to help me.

Let me insert here, that I did ask the Lord "What would you have me to do?" In a word, His response was GO!

As I recall the event, she drove, and I yelled out the car window for about twenty minutes. Then alas, a black furry critter, weighing about 40 pounds came darting towards the car. My eyes grew like large marbles. "There he is!" The dog probably couldn't believe his eyes.

We jumped out of the car like jack rabbits as I witnessed the very happy reunion of the dog and the owner. On the way home, I about burst into tears. My vocal cords were happy to be silent, and I know the neighbors must have been relieved as well.

Upon arriving back at her home, she was so appreciative of my willingness to help her out in this doggie dilemma. It was only as we got out of the car that she noticed that I was in my bed-time attire, my pajamas and robe. We laughed ourselves silly, and then I walked home.

As my adrenaline started to calm down, I asked the Lord to use this situation for "His glory and His purposes." Yes, He can and does use every tiny little thing we do for others.

To make a long story short, the following week I asked her to come to a Christmas program at our church. She came ... and heard about Jesus–Emmanuel ... God with us!

I don't know how God will use all of this in her life, but I considered it a joy to join in God's activity in my neighbor's life ... to let her know that God not only wants to "live within us," but to "help us and walk through" all the events of our lives.

When I finally came home from the excursion around the neighborhood, I got to thinking about why we looked high and low for that dog. The owner wasn't content to just call out his name and hope that he would come scurrying home. She knew the nature of her dog was to roam.

He had no intention of returning and, for a while, he enjoyed the freedom of wandering in new territory. But after the temperature came down and it got dark, things didn't look the same in his venture into freedom.

This made me think how God lovingly seeks after us. He knows our propensity to sin and to run away from Him and His ways. It's not in us to seek after God. He knows that, but because He loves us so much and longs to have a personal relationship with us, He comes looking for us through our lives and in our circumstances—as messy and lost as they are.

A few weeks later she had me over for tea, and when I knocked on the door, you can just about guess who welcomed me like never before. THE DOG! If dogs can piece together information, I can imagine his thoughts to be: *"That's the woman with the megaphone of a voice calling my name all over the neighborhood.... the night I was lost."*

My neighbor friend loved her dog. This furry critter was valuable to her and that's why she went looking for him. Because of her love she wanted the dog home.

In a similar way, it reminds me that God created each of us and we are loved, and are of value to Him, so *He works in our lives to help us "return home."* That's what it means to be saved ... Saved from our sin and its consequences.

Royalty in Rollers

It's time for a huge chuckle. So set your funny bone in place and prepare for hysterical laughter from this true event. It's been a long time since this scenario took place, but I remember it as though it happened last week.

My husband was born in Scotland and grew up in New Zealand. People from New Zealand and Scotland are, by nature, very hospitable. Now those cultures are a bit different from the culture in the United States.

My husband told me that when he was at school, he would often bring schoolmates over at various hours, and his mom would always share either biscuits (cookies) and tea or even a dinner with them.

Many times, people will use the phrase, "Next time you're in our area, stop by." I've found that although used rather frequently, it is not always sincerely spoken.

My husband travelled extensively in New Zealand and met many lovely people over the years. Being a small country, word spread that he and his wife were now living in Canada. Knowing him, he would have shared with most all the people he visited that if they were ever in our area, "please come and stay." There were no rules or understanding about calling first and seeing if it was convenient.

I hope you are getting the general tone of where this story is headed.

We had been married about three months when our "drop ins" (I mean visitors) began arriving. The phone would ring, and the accents on the other end would be a give-away that it was someone from New Zealand. My general response upon answering the phone was, "Are you at the airport, or bus depot? Sometimes their response would be "No, but we are flying tomorrow and wondered if you would be home for the next week or so?"

This new adventure-call came in the late afternoon. My husband answered the phone and voila, visitors from New Zealand. I have lost count of the number of couples we had enjoyed prior to receiving this call, so I was already familiar with the routine. In this instance, I gathered that they had already "arrived" and were hoping for transportation from the airport to their local accommodation—our home.

As usual, everything was going according to plan ... in response to the most recent call. My husband and I drove to the airport. He and I did not speak much on the way, and I wondered if there was more to this pick-up routine than expected. Was there ever!!!!!

He did manage to say, "There's something I need to tell you," In a kind of gentle warning. "What's wrong, or what do I need to know?" I cautiously inquired. Then the penny dropped, so-to-speak. It was then my husband told me about our arriving house guests ... and how I should "properly address" them.

The man should be addressed as Sir Peter Tait and his wife as Lady Tait. So, in the last few minutes before arriving at the airport my husband told me that our guest had been knighted by Queen Elizabeth II. This couple's soon-to-be accommodation was our very small home, three tiny bedrooms, and the only red carpet would be a tiny red throw rug.

Has your chin dropped to the floor yet? I mean, how would you feel with this up-to-the-minute news flash? Of course, I couldn't even answer. And any response given now would be meaningless since we were pulling into the airport. My husband encouraged me by saying they were very nice people, and he thought they would be easy to host for a few days. He didn't mention, however, that he only knew of them, but had never actually met them.

As I recall this adventure, I'm smiling from ear to ear as I know how the events took a joyful turn. At the time, I thought I could just hide somewhere and have a quiet little nervous breakdown, but since we were now at the airport, there just wasn't time. (Laughter!)

We pulled up to the arrivals area, and we quickly saw a pair of hands waving enthusiastically toward us. They were waiting patiently at curbside for their concierge service. They were very friendly, and most appreciative that we would be hosting them for a week as part of their vacation in Canada.

The nervous breakdown would just have to wait, and I remembered my instructions on how to greet them: "Sir Peter and Lady Tait." Got it! After our hugs and greeting, I began addressing them in the *proper manner*: "*Sir Peter and Lady Tait.*" It took less than two seconds and they told me to call them Pete and Lil from then on. Etiquette aside, that is what they wanted.

Everything was going well, and I even managed to produce an evening dinner. Our guests had an early-to-bed evening. The following morning, Lady Tait, or Lillian as I began calling her, arose and came out for breakfast. Her hair wasn't exactly perfectly groomed. She had a wonderful sense of humor, and we laughed at the mountain peaks her hair was in.

As we both laughed, I commented that I always enjoy working with other peoples' hair, such as putting hair in rollers, parking them under a dryer, and styling their hair. I felt safe enough to ask her if she wanted me to work with her disheveled peaks. She couldn't blurt out the affirmative fast enough.

So, after breakfast, Lady Tait and her new hairdresser went to work. We laughed and carried on like two little school girls, and when it was all over, she looked gorgeous and felt grateful. I was so thrilled that she allowed me this privilege of getting up close and personal to this member of royalty.

This couple visited us on a regular basis throughout the years, and I remember they stayed in almost every home we lived in for the next ten years. They even brought other couples with them. They are both at home with Jesus now. But I shall look forward to seeing them in heaven and reuniting with such fun and down-to-earth people.

It was a joy and delight to learn the lesson again and again to JUST BE YOURSELF, and to LOVE THOSE WHOM GOD BRINGS INTO YOUR HOME.

I also think that we should treat everyone who enters our homes like ROYALTY, because everyone needs to know that they are special because they are designed by God Himself.

Now, when are YOU coming to our home?????

A Wealthy Relationship

While on staff of a rather large congregation in the Southeast part of the United States, my husband and I were invited to a church dinner.

Personally, I'm not fond of head tables. However, at this event many guests had been invited and the seating arrangements were pre-assigned.

I viewed the scattering of place cards and my heart groaned–we were seated at the "display table" ... otherwise known as the "head table."

Quietly I asked the Lord if He was sure He wanted us at that table and that specific location. People began arriving and scurrying toward their assigned seats.

A few moments later, a lady came and began rearranging the cards as though they were on skates. Four cards were moved to a new location.

Now, I realize the Lord has something in mind. I kept a keen lookout as to where we were moving. And yes, we were still at the head table. The event was about to commence, so we settled into our assigned seats.

My heart wasn't happy, but as time passed, I began to recall that the Lord directs our steps ... our stops ... and even seats.

Soon we were in a pleasant conversation with the lovely couple seated next to me. They were simply delightful, and we seemed to just blend together as if we had known each other for years.

After dinner, my husband and I continued our interaction with them. They had about forty or more years of life experience on us, but that didn't matter at all.

We all seemed to enjoy one another so much that we wanted to continue this relationship.

Plans were made to go for dinner one evening. In fact, we had many dinner engagements with them. We loved being with them, and they seemed to enjoy our company as well.

We had only been married about four years, and financially we could pay our bills, but there wasn't much left over. If we ever went out for an evening, we needed to decide beforehand if we were going out for coffee … or ice cream because we couldn't afford both at the same time.

I trust you caught on to our "just making it … with not much left over."

One evening our new friends invited us out for dinner. It was to be a special evening. Little did I know 'how' special.

We were curious as we entered a building, and that we met in the lobby of a bank. We knew they had a drive-through at this banking facility, but it wasn't for serving food.

We followed them into the elevator. When the elevator door closed, it remained so for a very long time.

I can't remember the floor number, but we landed 'at the top.' Yes, the restaurant was at the top of this commercial high-rise building.

All of the restaurants we'd ever been to were at ground level, and so were the prices. The height of this restaurant and its commanding 360-degree view certainly suggested the prices were elevated as well. I'll get to that in just a minute.

Everyone was really dressed up. That means no jeans or slacks I might add. It turned out to be a private, very exclusive club.

After a few minutes of welcomed chit-chat, I began to look around. I didn't need to circle the entire environment before coming to my first observation.

Our names were on printed cards in front of us, and the cover on the pack of matches (black with gold lettering) had our friends' name on it. My eyes must have popped out like giant grapes at this observation.

This was nothing compared to my next revelation. My husband and I opened our menus at the same time and made the identical discovery. There were no prices next to the menu items.

This was no Bob's Big Boy, or Denny's, I assure you.

Our eyes met and you could almost read our thoughts appearing on our inner foreheads. This is incredible. Whenever we're invited out to dinner by anyone, we try and choose something that's reasonable on the menu.

With no prices, what were we to do? How could we make a sensible, conservatively-priced decision.

Our gentleman friend sensed our unease, and helped us relax by asking us to have 'whatever you like.' Needless-to-say, our dinner was incredible and we delightfully consumed every morsel on our plates.

Over the course of months, we had many meals with this couple. The problem was that they were always asking "us" out and not the other way around. By now, you may understand our dilemma.

We simply loved being with this couple, but at the time, we couldn't afford to even take them for a fast-food dinner.

One Sunday afternoon we picked them up at their penthouse condo on the beach and drove to our delicious ice cream destination—Baskin & Robins—yes, that's the 31-flavor ice cream chain for poorer folks like us.

I must have put in some overtime at the bank where I worked in order to afford this extravagance. I can't remember if they had one scoop or two, but their reaction to our ice cream social was certainly one of sincere appreciation.

Between licks of ice cream, we shared honestly and openly with our friends that we couldn't afford to reciprocate in the same fashion as they extended to us, but we really loved having them with us. They assured us that it was our friendship that was of "value" to them, regardless of the price of the cone.

We always had fun together. They weren't looking for our names on the cover of the matches. They just appreciated that we wanted to spend time with them, looking for nothing in return.

The Christmas season was fast approaching, and my husband and I wanted to have them over for dinner. We made plans for the evening and this couple seemed thrilled to be asked to our home.

Remember, these people lived at the top of a high-rise—a penthouse on the beach—that was much larger than the size of our home. We lived, shall we say, on the mezzanine level of the neighborhood.

The evening was set. Since we didn't have a dining room table, we borrowed a card table that had "several years' experience." I spread a white tablecloth, and did my best table presentation.

In case your curiosity is getting the best of you, no, there wasn't even a vase of fresh flowers on the table. We used the best and most down-to-earth approach—plates, serviettes (napkins), knife, fork and spoon, with salt and pepper on the side.

They arrived at our home and we were delighted. We escorted our friends into the dining room where our "dining table" was camouflaged in white accessories. The dinner conversation was laced with laughter, like it always had been when the four of us were together.

Since it was near Christmas, we wanted to give them a gift to show them love and how much we valued their friendship. The week before, I had made some homemade shortbread – probably about two dozen.

I wrapped the shortbread in a box, and then wrapped the gift as attractively as I could muster. I wanted the gift to look special, because I felt that the contents were "amazingly plain," just shortbread.

We finished our dinner and moved to the living room—just a few steps from the "dining table." They sat on our sofa and I presented the package to him. He opened it carefully and when he saw the contents, his eyes quickly moistened into tears.

Mine were not Mrs. Field's Cookies, and I was stunned at his tears. His wife was choked up as well. I will never forget what transpired after the grand opening of the box of shortbread.

I began to apologize in a quiet way for such an insignificant gift to them. Without being rude, he gently interrupted my apology with a response I was not expecting.

He used our names and said that they loved our friendship and were so pleased with our gift. They shared that our friendship was a "gift" to them.

I knew they were obviously very, very wealthy, and they could have spit us out as change as far as their mass of wealth was concerned.

But he quickly assured us that our friendship was precious and of great value to them.

They both began to share from their hearts that others they knew socially often tried to outdo them with dinners and lavish evenings.

Their other relationships were filled with people endeavoring to impress. My husband and I had nothing to impress them with ... except our love.

They both felt that our little box of cookies was the nicest gift they had ever received. I learned a valuable lesson from our friends that day. Never seek to impress anyone with anything less than your love for them.

Who knew that my reluctance in accepting God's placement at the "head table" would lead to such a lasting friendship?

Now, whenever I make shortbread, I'm often reminded that it's not the size of your table, or what you put on it, or even the gift you give, but the love that permeates the atmosphere.

It's how you make people feel that counts! And that can happen with a simple bowl of soup or a grilled cheese sandwich. So, who are you inviting for dinner?

An Honoring Gesture

At the time of this writing, we were still cautious in public due to COVID. The week prior we needed to visit our bank. We masked up before exiting the car and entering the bank. Funny that a few years ago, a person entering a bank wearing a mask would immediately be "suspect." As soon as we approached the teller, we noticed we were the only *masked* clients.

I was standing next to my husband, and soon noticed a young man ill at ease as he paraded back and forth and fidgeted with papers. His eyes were piercing, and his behavior was such that he was keen to stroke or poke at odd things near him.

From his appearance, I surmised him to be about 14 to 16 years of age, and assumed that he was just curious about the variety of materials on display around the teller area.

When I had worked at a bank many years ago, we had been schooled to be aware of people acting strangely. This young man certainly qualified. My attention was focused on him at this point, wondering why his behavior was a little odd.

In a while, it became clear that he was in the bank with an older gentleman, perhaps his dad. There was no conversation between the two of them, but every once in a while, this young man would glance over at the older man. Watching the two of them was like piecing together a puzzle. However, the pieces weren't yet clear as to their business at the bank.

After a few minutes, a female employee approached the older gentleman and informed him that he would need to wait a few minutes before being served as there were other customers ahead of him. Shortly after that, the young man moved over closer to this older man and sat down in a vacant seat.

Not long after, our teller advised my husband that we would need to be seated and wait for the bank manager to have a word with us. Now, we too were waiting for an appointment.

Since I didn't think we would have long to wait, I was okay to stand. However, as we entered the waiting area, the young man rose from his chair and glanced over at me. He began motioning with his hands for me to sit down in the chair he had occupied. Though he never spoke a word, he looked directly at me and continued pointing to the now empty chair.

I was suddenly uncomfortable, and since I had prepared myself for a short wait, this young man was making it a public display, and I wanted to remain standing.

Like the persistence of a policeman, this young man continued to glance my way and point. I can be slow at times, but it was now quite obvious that he wanted me to sit in the chair he had just vacated. I smiled and wagged my head in an east-west position indicating that I wasn't interested in sitting in the chair.

I did just use the word persistence to describe his actions, right? After several more points from this young man, I finally thought to myself, he means business. So, as not to cause any more stress to this young man, I "sat down." He smiled with delight and glanced away.

To our surprise, the older man said to us, "He doesn't talk," but did not tell us what prevented him from speaking. The last piece of the puzzle dropped into place.

This sweet-natured young man obviously noticed I was older than him, and he felt I should have the honor of being comfortable by sitting in that empty chair. A chair he could have chosen to remain in himself.

The puzzle picture came into view when I realized that God used this young man "to honor me." My eyes began to moisten. You may ask why. It was because I didn't see clearly enough to realize all the elements of this encounter.

God had chosen this boy who couldn't speak to bless me and show me He cared enough for my comfort.

Even now, as I write about this occurrence, there's a tender tug on my heart at the Lord's provision of rest, and how He chose to encourage someone with a disability to bless me.

God's love and kindness knows no bounds – whether it is evident through the sensitivity and kindness of this young boy, or perhaps a cup of tea with a friend, or even an act of service directed toward us. God made Himself known through the treasure of this young person's attentiveness to me.

Kindness is a Gift ... Sometimes Delivered without a Language

I was truly left speechless, but so filled with a quiet appreciation for how the Lord makes Himself known to us through sometimes simple, yet *unidentifiable* ways.

We often overlook the fact that our loving Heavenly Father is concerned about the "little details" of our lives.

Matthew 10:29 *"What is the price of two sparrows – one copper coin? But not a single sparrow can fall to the ground without your Father knowing it."*

Compassion – Up Close & Personal

If you dread the after-effects of anesthesia, you will appreciate some of the details about this post-surgery story. I realize that some people can awake from anesthesia and can slowly understand their surroundings, but I am not one of them.

This story will be short and sweet (poor word used here, I know), but the simple kindness of one friend overwhelmed me until I collected myself during the moments in which most people would have already left the recovery area.

We all know beforehand, that after any surgery, I'm *not* going to feel well. My stomach is just naturally configured to revolt at the invasion of sharp items on, or in my body. No need to go into details about the reason for the surgery, but I'll let your imagination fill in the blanks.

Just like going to an airport for a flight, you need to show up about two hours prior to the event – but in this case the trip is to the O.R. During this time, you are graced with a less-than-stylish "almost gown" that certainly did not receive rave reviews at the last, or any, European fashion show.

The preparation continues when a nurse arrives to play pincushion on your hand or arm in an attempt to get an IV started in your arm. Though not comfortable, all is as expected ... though in no way equivalent to first-class treatment on a flight!!

If you're alone, you begin scanning your surroundings – taking in all the details. Soon, a business-like Mr. Anesthesiologist enters your space and announces his title and explains the anesthetic procedure. He usually asks if you have any questions. By this point, your brain is still recovering from the fashion faux pas you are wearing – not to mention the IV connected to your arm. Most likely it is difficult to assemble your jumbled thoughts, while your memory has gone on vacation and forgotten to take you with it.

I appreciate anesthesiologists, but they sure are "powerful people" in their ability to night-night you at their chosen moment.

The following may cause you to believe that going to the OR is my preference over taking a vacation, since I carry a piece of paper into the hospital with me, which I give to the "night-night physician." Here's what it says:

DON'T FORGET TO GIVE ME THE ANTI-NAUSEA MEDS

For previous surgeries, my husband has always been allowed to stay with me until I'm taken into the surgical area. As I'm about to be carried via the hospital limousine–the gurney–I remind him of the following:

When I'm brought back to the room, make sure you have the ice cream bucket ready for me.

Once the attending doctor affirms everything is ready with an encouraging nod, I know that I'll be going "night-night" shortly. Some anesthesiologists give you a math test: count backwards from ten. I usually fail, because somehow the lights go out at around nine.

Apparently once the "put-you-out-doctor" leaves, your surgeon appears. The surgeon's fashion sense is much better than mine– for the moment, and he or she probably is all dressed in their best scrubs. For some reason the hospital staff is appropriately color coordinated!!

Somewhere in dreamland, I hear, "We're ready," and from that point on, I am too far gone to know anything about the bright little room, the sights, sounds, and smells… all for which I am quite happy.

Several hours usually pass and the limousine transports me from the post-op ICU to my room. It is here my consciousness begins to "kick" in … well … drift is more like it, and I am gradually alert enough to know that the surgery is over. I know that I'm alive and grateful… but my tummy is not cooperating, and things southward in my body are not peaceful. This is where I urgently request the "ice cream bucket." My husband calmly assures me that it's right by my side.

Just as the room is spinning back into focus, so are my predictions about being sick … and I was not a happy camper. Though my husband and a dear friend were present, they could do nothing as my insides rather rudely display their unhappiness about the event.

Of course, specific details are not necessary, but I do remember one remarkable aspect of that day.

While trying to position the ice cream bucket in a more agreeable location, I could see my friend at the edge of my vision. She knew I wasn't feeling well, and as my stomach was trying to "reestablish post-operative neutrality," shall we say, she would gently pat my shoulder, and say things like: "It's okay;" "try and get it all out," and "I'm here."

During all this, she was only about 6 inches from my face. Bless her for wanting to reassure me that I was "not alone." Her presence meant the world to me. To this day, I can close my eyes and see her up close and personal giving constant assurance. By the way, I am very glad she had a great grip on that ice cream bucket.

She continues to be a dear friend to me; one that I don't have to be at my best for her to love me. The experience was as if God

Himself came close and held me which *He did ... through the eyes and arms and tender words of my friend.*

Remembering the Losses of Others – Part 1

There are so many ways to tenderly touch the lives of people who have suffered. As I recall the experiences of others in this delicate and emotional area, I am still moved with compassion.

Almost all of us have experienced some kind of a loss in our life. Loss is a very real part of life, and can range from the loss of a friendship, a beloved pet, a dear friend, a family member, your country of origin.

Losses can also include intangibles including security, familiar surroundings, innocence, a job and much more. All losses touch our heart and stoke our emotions. Even more painful is that some pass through this journey seemingly alone. The Bible says in Galatians 6:2 "Bear one another's burdens."

Though being present with family and friends of the bereaved, attending a memorial service, sending flowers or a card are all commendable, there is more we can do. Let's focus on what transpires after the service—after the food and fellowship cease, and everyone goes back to their own routines.

It is hard to describe the quietness and emptiness of the home of the bereaved. What was once shared, now seems meaningless, and memories ebb ... just beyond one's grasp. Sometimes a scent or a sound triggers the memory of an event, but even that disappears almost as quickly in the stillness.

Several years ago, I had such a loss. Gone were the simple encounters that asked: "What's for dinner;" "How was your day;" "Would you like to go for a ride or a walk?"

It is possible to take advantage of amazing opportunities and make a difference in the life of someone who has experienced loss. At first, our seemingly full calendars may present an obstacle to reach out and get involved with someone. However, God has other ideas about these seasons in life.

It's amazing that we often have to experience something ourselves to gain insight. It is only when we have stubbed our toe, do we fully appreciate that reality. Walking through personal pain or loss sets the stage of understanding how to "tenderly touch" the life of another one going through a similar experience.

Remember, we all experience pain and grief differently. Believe me, I do not have a formula on all the ways we can lovingly help another through their pain and loss; but I do have a few ideas that I want to express in this delicate story.

It is easy to be around our friends and family when everything is "just fine" and enjoy those times together. Our conversations are genuine as is our happiness. However, in all honesty, we shy away from those who have experienced a loss, adjustment, or disappointment. I know I can feel that way sometimes.

As a caregiver for my mother, I missed frequent social connections. As a result, my interactions with others were often awkward, which I later viewed from "God's perspective." Humanly, we usually don't know what to say or to do, though we wish we could just take away their pain ... but cannot.

God has introduced me to a new thought about this. The first being, "This isn't about you.... it's about the *other* person." I think all of us can agree that we're often so focused on ourselves, that we forget about the other person.

Over and over in life, God seems to say to me, "It's not about you!" If we want God to use us in the life and loss of another, our focus needs to be on faithfully and practically loving on that person.

By way of introduction, here are a few suggestions that have breathed freshness, tenderness, laughter and love into hearts that are hurting. These have been woven into my own life through my own journey, and have touched the lives of others.

Though I cannot *take away someone's pain*, I can enter into their life's experience "of pain" and touch them in tender, practical ways by being the "hands and feet" of our caring Jesus to them.

Here are a few instances of social disconnection:

- Someone diagnosed with an incurable disease
- Someone who is a caregiver 24/7
- Someone who has lost a spouse
- Someone preparing for, or recovering from major surgery

Let me share just a few of the ways God has encouraged me to "journey" with friends who have walked a very difficult and emotional journey.

One dear friend lost his wife. He was a retired pastor who visited those preparing for, or recovering from surgery. He was there at their "pre-op" time to pray with them. He was there when some lost their spouse.

But when this man's wife went home to heaven—very few reached out to him. People just didn't know what to say.

In life, there are situations when there "are just no words." It is simply our presence that means the world to someone. Each morning or evening I would phone him to just say hello. Our conversation was short, and I'd ask a range of questions at various times. Sometimes I would ask what he had for dinner or lunch.

Most of all I'd ask him daily, how do you feel today, and would "just listen." But most often I would just say, "Hello, I'm thinking about you and I care." *It wasn't what I said, but more often how I listened and chose to just be in contact with him.*

Listening is a *wonderful ministry* and a lovely way of telling others you love them, because you don't have to *"know anything… just listen."* Now for me, that's a freedom I can embrace.

People just need us to walk **"with them"** through their loss and grief. People need us to "talk and reminisce about their loved one." People need to know that even though their loved one has gone … most importantly, they are not forgotten. People love to hear us "join them in discussion" about their departed loved one.

I recall one such couple who lost their son through a very difficult challenge. My husband encountered the father while shopping, and stopped to ask about his son who had now been gone for ten years. The man broke into tears and they entered into a heart-felt discussion about his loss. My husband asked him if others would get into a tender dialogue with him about the life of his son.

The man shared that hardly anyone would ask about his treasured son. His tears were fresh, not because he hadn't worked through the grieving process, but because my husband had taken the time to ask about his dear son.

We may feel uncomfortable about asking about others' losses, but their heart will know and be grateful that we cared enough to ask. It's not about us, but about "them". Several grieving friends have said that most people never bring up the name of their deceased loved one because they're afraid that it will cause more pain. *That couldn't be more wrong.* Remembering shared experiences, keeps their loved one's memory alive and helps them in the grieving process.

One dear friend said that my calls every day was something she could count on. She knew she wasn't forgotten. Most all of the friends I have called do not live in the city where my husband and I reside. So, this is "long-distance caring."

Remembering the Losses of Others – Part 2

If you live near enough to a friend, perhaps a note, a casserole, a banana loaf is always meaningful. If possible, include them once a week for dinner.

Many years ago, we had a neighbor who lost his wife and we'd have him over for dinner, or a snack, and even watched TV together occasionally to get him out of his house.

He shared that he felt so connected to others who cared. What you serve them doesn't matter as much as the fact that you cared enough to *"include them."*

We all have responsibilities and time restraints. Sharing your baked goods, a meal, or just spending time with someone who is grieving is wonderful.

Your frequent "check in" calls may last only four or five minutes, but can make all the difference in the world to a person in a painful season ... for that day, that week or that month. Your *"five-minute ministry"* is not a huge commitment, but creates a special bond between you and that one special person.

After my friend had gone to be with the Lord, the daughter of the pastor I used to call each day, said: "He told me that your calls every day were his lifeline." I had phoned him daily until God took him home. Our small exercise of love and refreshment to others causes us to be refreshed ourselves.

Consider caring for caregivers who need care too! Reaching out to a care-giver can help them in their role of love to those they're caring for. God sent me two lovely women who "gifted me" with their time and talents.

One woman came every week and attended to a number of practical needs such as household chores, preparing lunch for my mom, or even surprising me with dinner in the oven. My mother loved having her around, and it gave me a refreshing break for a couple hours to rest or have a long walk.

Another friend would visit my mother and me every week. She was especially creative in the garden where she would arrange flowers beautifully. Honestly, she could arrange a handful of dandelions as though they were roses.

She would frequently bring a bouquet of flowers to my mother.

She and her husband supported me through my care-giving role by phoning me, coming over for lunch, decorating our home at Christmas. Each week, she would share of herself in a variety of practical ways including listening to my fears without any judgment.

It was a time when I needed a friend and had nothing to give in return. After my mother went home to heaven, they listened to my memories of my mother for a year and half.

Through simply listening to our friends' stories and memories over and over *and over,* we assist them through their grieving process. In reality, we never really "get over" our losses; we "get through them." When a person has a relationship with God, they receive a deep and real comfort which is sometimes brought to us through others. We all mourn some kind of loss—whether human or otherwise.

Through our "tender touches," we actually love others who may be dealing with loss, loneliness or headed heavenward. In essence, we *"walk them home."*

I like to tell new acquaintances that I'm the type of friend that can enjoy a bologna sandwich on the curb just to enjoy another's company. Now, I always need to be that kind of friend to others.

There is another way to love someone who is grieving by remembering that "DATE" on the anniversary of the loss. Many have shared with me that the anniversary date brings with it a "tremendous" emotion and a full sense of the reminder of what took place.

I have a couple of precious people in my life that I have marked on "my calendar" the date of "their loss." I phone them on that date and let them know that I'm remembering "with them." A friend shared with me that when I remember that date with them, she feels her grief is lessened and held in the heart of another.

In one of the neighborhoods we lived, there was a Christmas gathering. Most all of the surrounding neighbors were invited. I remember vividly the day a neighbor lady walked through the door. She seemed a friendly happy person. For some reason, I was drawn to her and thought to myself, "I'd like to get to know her…, but had no idea how that was going to happen as I wasn't aware of any of her interests."

Well, God did!

I found myself listening intently to what she enjoyed talking about. It wasn't long before she shared with me that she was alone. Her husband had died two years ago, and it was still a painful emotion for her, especially at Christmas time, as that wasn't far away from the anniversary of her husband's death.

Oddly enough, she shared the date of his passing with me in conversation. My immediate reaction inwardly was to "remember that date."

Soon after leaving the party, I went to my calendar and marked down the date she gave me. I prayed, and asked the Lord how could I let her know that I cared about her pain? I'm accustomed to walking our dogs in the neighborhood every day. The moment I came around the corner where she lived, it "dawned on me" what to do—write a note and put it in this woman's mail box on the anniversary date.

I prepared the card and put the date of delivery in the upper right-hand corner of the envelope (in pencil of course). Early that morning I made the "*delicate delivery.*" Within just a few hours I got a "teary telephone call" from her telling me how much my wee note meant to her. She made the comment that it seemed like God put that note in her mailbox for just the appropriate moment.

Well, in a sense, God did just that. I was His mail carrier that day.

There is no "greater joy" than to be the hands and feet of our living Savior. Our lives are filled with "*Divine opportunities" waiting for our participation.* It's allowing God to order the agenda of our activity each day, and living our lives with "intentionality!"

If we're willing, He is full of surprises that will lead us into the hearts and lives of others, if we're willing.

It's a "*quiet ministry*" to be sure, but one that holds the heart of your friend who has experienced a loss ever-so-gently and with heart-felt compassion.

Kindness is love in action ... OUR ACTION!

Making a Difference When you Least Expect It

It was just before Christmas; and a story about a tiny gift given to a very small and colorful recipient comes to mind.

I was in the yard cleaning up weeds and tidying up. We were living in a place with a warm, arid climate, and while passing the small fountain in our yard, I noticed the water had been evaporating quickly.

Just prior to flooding the fountain's container, I noticed my favorite color of "red" floating in the water. I stooped down to investigate what could possibly be in the water, and realized it was a tiny little Lady Bug.

Please understand that I do NOT speak lady bug, but if I did, I am sure if I would have heard: "Pick me up and let me off this ocean of water." At least that was my interpretation of this little one's predicament.

Since time was of the essence, with my right hand I scooped this Miss Lady out of the pond of death. I am sure if my hearing and lady bug-to-English translation abilities were better, I would have heard a giant "Thank You!" from this tiniest of creatures.

I looked around for a somewhere to place her safely. To my right a leafy shrub appeared perfect. Within seconds she had probably cleared her airways and moved her tiny little legs. Her body paused for only about ten seconds, and off she walked.

I stood still with my heart engulfed in delight at the small act of kindness which saved the life of this helpless lady bug. We need to stop and look for small "divine opportunities" to MAKE SOMEONE'S DAY. Turning from the fountain, I was overcome with this sense of a profound truth washing over me.

It's especially wonderful when our small acts of kindness are performed anonymously. You know the ones—where we react to opportunities immediately in front of us, and there's no time to be thanked for our small gesture of thoughtfulness.

In our life there are so many opportunities to make a tiny difference in the lives of others that come along by extending grace, love, and kindness to both human and animal.

Okay, back to the Christmas season; shouldn't we be kind and loving to others who may be yearning for some kindness? Perhaps a smile, or giving up a parking spot at the shopping mall? However, what about the rest of the year? There will always be opportunities – often in *unexpected ways on unexpected days* to reach out and share a smile or a gentle touch to another.

Before wrapping up this story as my gift to you, I will share two experiences that occurred at a local shopping mall. While stopped at our local grocery store at the mall, I encountered two wonderful "divine appointments."

Before I entered the supermarket, I was walking toward a beautiful woman who was coming toward me. Perhaps in her 90's, she was nicely groomed from head to toe, and looked so pretty and fresh in her chosen attire. I couldn't help but approach her and tell her, "You look stunning!" Her eyes grew big and a radiant smile encompassed her face. I could almost see a tear in her eye. She gratefully expressed a "Thank you."

I couldn't get over her next comment. "I'm an older woman, and I never get that kind of a response from anyone." I quickly added, "Honey, when another woman says you look stunning, you look stunning." From the look on her face, I think I made her "year."

What a joy that was for me to share that with her.

I entered the grocery with only a single item on my list. I quickly grabbed my item and headed for the checkout where the people ahead of me all seemed to have about twenty-five things. Since no one glanced my way to see that I had only ONE ITEM, I was not given an opportunity to go ahead of them. I sighed and prepared for the wait in line.

I heard a sudden commotion behind me. An older woman had fallen and people were scrambling to help her. As I turned around, the next moment I found myself holding the woman's shoulders asking if she was in pain. I then asked whether she was on any medication, etc. Within sixty seconds, and with the help of two others, she was lifted to her feet and grateful for her three "body lifters."

All seemed well and everyone drifted away, but I felt the need to remain and walk with her through the checkout line. By this time, we were verbal friends, and we walked out of the mall and into a medical clinic just to check out her vitals. She assured me she was fine, and I left her in the good hands of a nurse who assured me she would take care of this nice lady.

Upon leaving the medical office, I realized I had left the item which I had gone to purchase on a counter at the grocery store. I headed back to where I had left my item, and waited again. After paying and walking out, my eyes caught the smiling face of my new "mall friend." She was sitting comfortably in the lounge area of the mall while waiting for her ride home.

As our eyes met, I rushed over to where she was seated. We embraced as though we were long-time friends. She looked beautiful and appeared physically fine. It must have been a frightening experience to fall over your grocery bags when you're in your "young eighties" while standing in line.

I felt privileged to have been in her path when she fell so that, along with others, we could assist with loving support for this woman in her time of need.

Oh, the opportunities are endless, once we open our eyes and hearts ... and make ourselves available for God's use in any "ordinary" way. This is all the more relevant when this need interrupts our day to fulfill a higher purpose in the life of another.

Most of my Jesus-led interactions with others have been very "ordinary." I love sharing that truth, because many expect doing something for God means doing so in a *significant* or *spectacular* manner. Holding to such an unfounded expectation will cause you to miss Him in the daily. God's love for each one of us shows up in His intentional care of the tiny, intimate details of everyday living.

So, yes, I gave thanks to Jesus for "interrupting my space in line" to be used on behalf of another.

I wonder who might need "you" in the coming day

The Gift of Our Words:
The Expression of Our Heart!

Though we have all heard the expression, "*A picture is worth a thousand words,*" but what does that mean? For me, it's when I see something so lovely, so heart-warming, and so delightful that it moves my heart beyond a verbal statement. We hear people try to describe an event as "that's beyond description," or "I just can't find the words."

I was recently thinking about *words*. The words we hear and the words we speak. The word itself is a one syllable collection of letters that carries meaning: W O R D S. Our words can carry a tremendous weight in and of themselves. They can bring joy, encouragement, and delight; but they can also transmit disappointment, discouragement, disillusionment, and destruction.

Words can either create a "construction zone" or a "demolition site." The elements of speech that proceed from our mouths have the potential to deliver affirmation or devastating criticism. It's not just "what we say," but "how we say it" that can bless and strengthen the heart of another, or demoralize them in a split second.

Words convey expression from our hearts. There is one collection of words that may seldom be used, but words with a message that is tenderly and longingly sought after; and those are the words **I LOVE YOU.**

Sadly, I have often heard people share that their parents never said those words to them. They knew their parents loved and cared for them, but the parents found it difficult to let the words proceed from their lips to their children. Often culture, background, or how people are raised can squelch that loving expression.

I think back to the many people who have encouraged, instructed, corrected, and loved me during my life. They stretched my character to grow and think about others ahead of myself. People who have accepted me, just as I am (warts and all), and loved me beyond measure, seeing potential in me that I never comprehended in myself.

God has used such a carrousel of delightful people to bless my life here on earth. He has orchestrated a "lifetime array" of circumstances, during which I have been introduced a wide variety of people who loved, taught, and mentored me.

At the end of last year, I wanted to express to a few precious friends how "grateful" I was that they had been part of my journey through time here on earth. Their lives touched and enriched me in ways they probably never realized. My heart and life have experienced such nourishment, enthusiasm, encouragement, correction, and joy because of the many "ways and words" these people have shared and they have had a profound impact upon my heart and life.

The last few weeks I've experienced encouraging comments from five friends that related to a few short responses I gave them in a text. I was delighted to affirm each person, but was surprised by their "appreciative comments" on how I phrased my affirmation. What an awakening to me reminding me again that how we *craft our comments and conversation* can not only be helpful, but sometimes life-changing by giving others a fresh perspective.

Our lives "impact and influence" others around us. I was especially thinking of the impact of our words! We deposit positive and life-giving joy and encouragement to others, not just by *"what we say,"* but *"how we say it,"* and sometimes, by what we choose *"not to say!"*

For me, I struggle inside when I'm around "opinionated" people. And I need to be careful here, because my own mouth and tongue can "motor" around on the highway of expressing unsolicited opinions.

No need to take notes, but let me share how God addressed something ugly in me a few months ago. My scripture reading that particular morning (Proverbs 29:11) is presented in a few translations below:

- "*A fool vents all his feelings, but a wise man quietly holds it back.*" RSV
- "*A fool utters all his mind: but a wise man keeps it in till afterwards.*" KJV
- "*A fool lets it all hang out; a sage quietly mulls it over.*" Message

Oops, you might be saying, I'm not a fool. Well, God seems to call a spade a spade. Or on a clearer note, He calls sin ... exactly what it is, sin. Sometimes our words *can* be categorized as words that proceed from a foolish tongue.

My eyes caught on the word *fool*. I didn't want to linger there, but God was kindly pointing out that there was a better way to handle people and circumstances in life. There was a boomerang affect when I read the rest of the verse. "*... but a wise man holds it back.*" Holds **WHAT** back?

At first, perhaps like you, I wasn't fond of the word *fool*. God loves us "just as we are;" but He loves us too much to "leave us there." I wondered what a wise man holds back or refrains from. Yes, part of that verse (in other translations) uses the word anger. But He's not just referring to holding in the wrong kind of anger. Anger is an emotion for sure, but anger most often is reflected in our *WORDS* and *WAYS* with others and towards others.

Here's a verse that addresses the formula for "holding back our words," and I've memorized this verse to help me be watchful in what I say.

> *"The heart of the righteous studies how to answer, but the mouth of the wicked pours forth evil."* Proverbs 15:28

If you're convicted in any way here, please get in line *behind me* on this one! Let's learn together. What captured my thinking was this: this applies to not only anger, but anything that's "on your mind." It wasn't long before the word "opinion" came into view.

So often if I have an opinion about something, I feel it needs to be "let out of its cage." After reading this verse in Proverbs 29:11, I looked at the bottom section of my Jeremiah Study Bible where there's a further explanation of the meaning of certain verses.

I mentioned my "discomfort" earlier when I'm around opinionated people (who seldom see themselves this way); and I was blown out of my socks when God's arrow fell right on *my turf*. I can be opinionated too. Yes, it even hurts as I express this in writing for all the world to see, but many times it was true of me.

So, I committed the verse to memory to help ward off the temptation of voicing what "I think about a topic" without an invitation to do so. My new trains of thought are to:

"Zippa da lippa." Or perhaps, *"Engage mind before stepping onto the accelerator of my tongue."* Just because I have an opinion doesn't mean it needs expression. I've found that we "seldom, *if ever*, have *all the facts* about a matter, anyway."

That being said, many things are better left unspoken, and unless asked, hold on to our opinions.

So, in summary, I'm choosing to continue to study "how to answer" as well as "how to **not** answer." How about you? Our text book on this should be the Bible, not the dictionary. Just in the book of Proverbs alone, there are numerous verses that teach a willing student how to interact and connect with others in a "grace-filled" manner.

Jesus was a "Master communicator," and He longs for His children to enlist in His "communication class" as willing students. I've been in His class for a few years now. If you feel uneasy in this area, I would love to have you join me, so I don't feel that I'm the only one in this "Carefully Crafted Communication Class."

If you're not certain that God has a lot to say about this area of our "speech," I have a 31-day challenge for you. Since there are 31 chapters of Proverbs, there's a chapter for every day of the month. When you're reading each chapter (s l o w l y) circle every word that appears that refers to speech, words, lips, tongue, etc. You get what I mean.

Perhaps you'll be as shocked as I was. But then again, how marvelous that God would want to challenge what we say and how we say it. He offers a "free education" so we're more effective with His Word and our ways with others.

> "The heart of the wise *teaches his mouth*, and *adds learning* to his lips." Proverbs 16:23

Oh, that our words and opinions be filled with expressions of encouragement, sound counsel, and filled with grace. Will you join me in "cutting the kindling" so only goodness is ignited.

> "Where there is *no wood*, the fire goes out; and where there is no talebearer, strife ceases." Proverbs 26:20

Before I "stop writing" (ha ha ha), let me share a moment I had while in my car with another driver on the highway of life. I don't recall the exact details, but suffice it to say that I made a poor judgement in a parking lot. I was made painfully aware that my judgement wasn't the best. How do I know that? The driver gave me a piece of his mind that he couldn't afford to lose. His words and hand gestures just about tore me to pieces. This man's words just came bulldozing out of his mouth, I felt buried. He got out of his car and headed towards me. This gave me a moment to draw a quick breath of prayer as God brought to my mind Proverbs 15:1.

I can only give credit to Jesus for literally filling my mind and heart with the words in that verse that I had memorized. Once he was within ear-shot of my voice, I found myself *apologizing* for my error in judgement. Yes, you read that correctly. I apologized! I told him I was in the wrong and so very sorry.

By now, I probably have your full attention, and you're wondering how this turned out. Right?! My comment literally took him by shock and surprise. He didn't know whether to eat a banana or crawl back into his car. Once he gained his "composure," he gently said something like, "Oh, that's okay." Then off we travelled in our separate directions. I'll never forget the power of God's word in that automobile scenario.

> "A soft word turns away anger, but a harsh word stirs up wrath." Proverbs 15:1

Remember, our words are either a "*construction zone*" or a "*demolition site*" in the lives of others. Let's be wise and positive in our speech, building others up and offering grace to them as God is building His character in them, as well as us.

Years ago, Ruth Bell Graham, wife of evangelist Billy Graham, saw a sign by the road: *"End of Construction—Thank you for your patience."* Smiling, she remarked that she wanted those words on her gravestone.

Uncluttering Our Hearts: Finding Balance in our Values, Priorities & Activities

My mom used to say that whatever opportunity came up in school my hand shot up before I ever knew what the task was. With that in mind, I'd like to travel back in time and invite you into my heart.

Once at a summer camp, volunteers were being sought, and I still suffered from "hand*itus*" disease. Camp organizers needed someone to attend to the *John* at the camp.

At 15, this sounded interesting! That is until I was introduced to my new assignment – the *John* was the "boy's bathroom." I was not a happy camper, and it was the beginning of toning down my "enthusiastic willingness."

As people, we are often controlled by our will, emotions, and thoughts. Through life we are also accompanied with three external constant companions: VALUES, PRIORITIES, and ACTIVITIES.

These three companions direct our interests and involvement – essentially our direction.

As with any journey into uncharted areas, it is always helpful to start with a point of reference or true NORTH. Once Jesus is chosen as Master or Lord, He becomes our North, and our three travel companions then prepare us for the journey ahead.

However, if our journey does not have a stable point of reference – you know – Jesus being our NORTH, it is quite likely we will wander aimlessly seeking both stability and direction.

For many years, my true North was rooted in activity.

Recent advancements in technology have simply made our active lifestyles busier. Our full day–timers were once badges of social acceptance but quickly consumed every spare moment of our lives.

Many people are actively frustrated ... fruitlessly living to find God's purpose and His kingdom. Activity doesn't mean productivity. In seeking the Lord's priority, there are times in which we have to discern and determine what He doesn't want us to do. That can be as hard as it is sometimes in knowing what He does want us to do.

Perhaps, like me, you have said "yes" even before someone finished asking you to do something. On the surface I was extremely active. I was the human dynamo, and boy was I busy. However, my life was empty – and barren.

At this time in my life, I found great fulfillment in being busy and needed, and of course there was always something to do! My entire being moved from one commitment to another, and relaxation was out of the question!

My need to be needed overtook my life, and my precious family fell to the bottom of my priority list. My quiet time with the Lord simply became a checklist item – another event squeezed in-between other responsibilities.

My activities, like weeds, were choking the "life and relationship" I needed to have with God.

It was during this time that God allowed and used difficult circumstances to get my attention. One day while lying on the sofa because I was literally burned out, I heard a Godly man on the radio speak about the "busyness" of life. His concluding remarks brought me upright on the sofa: "If you're too busy to pray, you're too busy!"

I was troubled and knew I needed to make some changes. God helped me realize that I had allowed the needs of others to orchestrate and dictate my life's responsibilities and activities.

I finally saw that just because there were needs, I wasn't the one destined to meet every one.

I had struggled with saying "yes" to God's assignments, and "no" to others. In my mind it was because I wanted to help and be involved in others' lives, but in reality, a greater void in my heart was being filled with activity, and that often was at the expense of my home and health.

How often had I done things to overcome my own insecurity – just so that I would be recognized, praised or included?

God's Word wonderfully and powerfully helps us see through the "lens of His eyes," His perspective. Sadly, I saw that I was saying *"yes to everyone, but Him."* I was allowing *"my need to be needed"* to dictate my real responsibilities and priorities.

It was then, God brought my focus to my day–timer which allowed me to identify how my schedule would align with His plans for me.

God began with my attitude about serving Him. He helped me realize I had been working "for Him" and not "with Him." It was through painful discoveries that I found that I had it backwards.

"My" calendar was full of tasks and plans, and then generously sprinkled with requests to God to bless them. I had been just too busy to listen to God – often merely reading His Word and then closing the book.

At the time, my heart cried out: "God, I can't seem to see you and detect your activity in my life."

God used a stranger on a radio program to point this out. Only then was I ready to hear some wisdom in the area of "listening to and for God."

This stranger said that if I wanted to hear God's voice in my inner being, I NEEDED TO TURN DOWN THE VOLUME OF MY LIFE. If God had wanted to contact me, my busy life would have returned an "all circuits are busy" message, and His call may have ultimately gone to "voice mail."

God is usually not in the habit of shouting above the roar of activity with which we surround ourselves.

My busyness had taken on a life of its own, and needed constant attention to stay afloat. Hardly ever taking time to just "breathe and relax," my mind was continually preoccupied.

The continual flurries of activity never ceased, and were rendering me spiritually fruitless. I realized that I was the only one responsible for eliminating them.

It was at this time that God got "down to business with me." Since God is more concerned with *character* rather than *connection*, His methodology seldom uses *instant gratification* – you know, the very heart of social media.

My continual "pedal to the metal" life had been creating a roar of activity through which I could barely hear His voice or feel His gentle promptings.

I understood my need to "eliminate distractions" bulldozing me to the point of overload, and soon I was spending more time in my daily marinating time with God, and my day-timer started to take on a "fresh new look."

Basically, it's learning to walk "with Him" and not "ahead of Him." This meant asking God to sift through the requests being made of me, and allow Him to indicate whether I accept or graciously decline. These passages from Proverbs 4:20, and 3:6 were the start of that journey: "Ponder the path of your feet, and let all your ways be established." "In all your ways, acknowledge Him, and He shall direct your paths."

We live before an audience of One, and like you, I want to hear His "well done!" In essence, God's cares more about *who I am BECOMING*, rather than *what I am doing for Him*.

My insecurity finally allowed me to understand that He adores you and me – just the way we are ... warts and all. He wants us to be fruitful, thereby eliminating our need to continually post on social media.

Alas, social media maven, Annie All-together, who spends hours daily posting her every move so that her 985 "friends" can stay updated on her perfect, put–together life is simply not living in reality.

If our desire is to please our Lord and hear from Him, we do not need to do everything. If we were, we become like the performer who has to keep multiple plates spinning lest they come crashing down. Why? He is simply trying to impress others.

Like books, our lives should have margins – space to give our eyes relief from constant words. Life margins are needed so we won't become overwhelmed and overcommitted.

Margin is simply a byproduct of living in sync with our Savior's schedule according to the Scriptures. To find margin we need a Messiah who gives us instruction for both labor and rest."

I am convinced that Satan's easiest tactic is to "keep us distracted and too busy," so we don't have time to get our life in line with God. Once we are correctly positioned with our true North, God provides us with our individual GPS, *GOD'S POSITIONING SYSTEM*.

However, like the phone app, God only gives us one instruction at a time, and waits until that is done; then you receive another instruction.

What is clear now is that *"If I'm too busy to pray...I'm too busy."* After God, my family should be my first priority. As appealing as ministries and opportunities may sound, if not instigated or orchestrated by God, they can easily overwhelm us.

By taking time to talk to God about our activities and involvements, we give Him the opportunity to "influence us ... our heart and mind."

Consider what happens when we consume garlic, we don't need to announce it! It "oozes" from our pores. Similarly, being in the center of His "direction" allows us to ooze Jesus into everything we do. We'll be "contagious with Christ."

I have found some very helpful and practical "sieve questions" that I pour through whenever I'm asked to be involved in an activity. I'd like to share them with you:

- Has God asked me to be involved here?
- Has He said anything about this in His Word?
- Do I have a quiet inner peace about "doing whatever?" Or, do I feel pressured to do it?
- Will this involvement be in keeping with His priority for my life?
- Will this involvement take me away from family responsibilities/priorities too much?
- Will this involvement keep me too busy to have "quality time with Him?"
- If you're married, is my spouse "on board" with me taking on this commitment?
- Is this in keeping with my "giftedness?"

These questions give me a "clear idea" of whether I should say yes, or no. I love God's kindness in helping me recognize this and reduce my self-imposed stresses.

I am still learning the "disciplined art" of saying "yes" to God and "no" to any activity He wasn't asking me to join.

My calendar is in continual transformation, but since His working in this area of my life years ago, my day timer and clogged spiritual arteries have taken on a new and refreshed direction. My activities and priorities look different, because He is helping me to evaluate them from His vantage-point.

You can finish this sentence: "If we don't come apart and be with Him ... there's a good chance we will simply ... _____"

To summarize this process of uncluttering our hearts, let's look again at our three lifelong travel companions – Values, Priorities and Activities, in light of putting Jesus first in our lives:

Our VALUES determine our PRIORITIES

Our PRIORITIES determine our ACTIVITIES

Our ACTIVITIES determine our HEART-BEAT

So, how is your calendar looking?
For Whom is your heart beating?

Not in My Lifetime!

The Germination of a Plan

I can't trace the moment I sensed God's alternate plan for us, but it likely started nine months earlier, through the loss of one of our "furry pets." Winnie, our little Pomeranian, had a number of seizures, and out of kindness, we had to say goodbye to her. For you pet-lovers, you'll know how difficult that was. We know they are pets and only animals, but try and convince our hearts of that.

Not long after, we joyfully welcomed my sister-in-love (not law) Linda, to our home after she experienced the deep grief of her son going home to be with the Lord. We were thrilled that she agreed to come, rest, and allow us to exercise the oxygen of His love into her life as He comforted and sustained her throughout her many emotional adjustments.

We loved having her and enjoyed many days and evenings chatting, laughing, and recalling family stories and the various avenues of challenge and change in her life and in ours. I clearly recall her comments regarding her decision to move to Australia. Yes, we could see and enjoy the thought of "her" move and personal transition.

Though she often said, "Wouldn't it be wonderful if you would move there too?" My spirit was not entirely in agreement whenever she said this, and I likely muttered something under my breath… and what does all this tell you? That God sees and knows all, even the things said under our breath.

Linda began to feel more settled in her thinking and emotions, and shared that she felt God was releasing her from our love and home and was leading her to Australia. She and my husband spent hours on the internet, looking for, and eventually finding a nice comfortable, cozy and safe place into which she could move, and it was on Australia's Gold Coast. The price was right and an offer was accepted.

So about five months after enjoying her stay with us, she boarded an Air Canada flight to Brisbane, Australia and the rest is history. We soon settled back into our routine without her.

A Second Blow

Four months later, we realized that our 15-year-old Papillon, Chelsea, was suffering the effects of her age and health. She quickly began to take a turn for the worse, and soon she too was gone. Through God's kindness, He showed us it was time to say good-bye in the kindest of ways. I will stop here to have a cry, but I'll be back, because this transitional story is just beginning to page itself in writing.

Over the years my husband, Peter, has travelled often while I've been content to remain at home. However, after the latest loss of a cuddly, furry friend, I did not wish to remain home for his next three-week trip to China and India.

Though I had friends and neighbors nearby and could have visited to my heart's content while my husband was away … my heart would "not settle!" To put it plainly—I had to get out of the house!

This was certainly not normal for me to even consider subjecting myself to a 14-hour flight to another country all by myself, but the need to get away was strong. I chose Australia because I knew Linda lived there, and I would be welcomed in her home where I could settle my emotions. My husband booked the trip, and I was off in less than three weeks.

At the end of October, 2016, I left for Australia. In hindsight, looking in my personal rear-view mirror, the purpose of the trip is abundantly clear now, but at the time, it made absolutely NO SENSE whatsoever.

While packing for the trip, I had chosen a book about Joseph (a Biblical young man), but at the last hour, I changed my mind and chose a book about Esther, by Chuck Swindoll. This is an important factor for the rest of this story.

Modern travel is like entering a large time capsule, and several hours later you and 300 others arrive in a different time zone and country. Arriving in Australia was a tremendous delight, and I will skip many details of this trip, and its many surprises.

After a day of adjusting to the time difference, Linda took me for a lovely lunch the following day with some new neighbor-friends who had reached out to her. During the course of the lunch, I was asked how I met my husband.

This was an incredible opportunity to share with these ladies how God invaded my heart and life's journey to bring about a love-story and marriage to a man who had left his home -country of New Zealand and travelled to Canada. A year later, he found himself in my "home town" of Columbus, Ohio. I briefly shared the many incredible details of how God brought us together. Later I thought, perhaps the trip to Australia was just for the purpose of sharing about the Lord in that delightful, glass-covered garden restaurant.

LEARNING FROM ESTHER

In the following two weeks, while studying the book I had brought along, I was also introduced to Esther from the Bible. God had prepared her for something great, and it was part of His plan for saving His people, Israel. The author, Chuck Swindoll, wrote about her journey with God and this message captivated me *daily*. Little did I know, that God's ideas and plans for my husband and me were proceeding much the same way.

Over the years, using a journal has helped me see God's sovereign hand directing my circumstances and weaving those circumstances into His plan. Now, while reading about Esther's life, I slowly and steadily saw a sentence here and there that captured my thoughts. It seemed that each day I felt drawn into her story and something was unfolding daily that I just *couldn't explain*.

Daily, as I read about Esther and her willingness to just obey God in the "tiny details" and live out the integrity of her life before others, my thoughts and gleanings from the book built on the previous comments entered in my journal. Each day there was a list of ideas about God's will in moving you out of the comfortable and safe places of your life.

Then there came the day about GOD'S SURPRISE. It began as a thought: "*What would you do if God's will "surprised you?*" Like most of you, I enjoy the safety of the known and comfortable. I was now about two thirds through the book, and my heart began to get uneasy. From that point on, it "seemed" like God was about to turn my life upside down.

Throughout reading the book on Esther, I was introduced to and became friendly with another woman in the neighborhood. She had an engaging personality and was just fun to be around.

In Australia, a Villa is a term referred to in this neighborhood to describe a condo. My new friend owned a Villa. This new term would soon be part of my regular vocabulary. Our conversation turned to her desire to sell her place and move to another one-story home.

What was strange was that though I loved my neighborhood and neighbors, and was quite "at home" in Canada, that I was drawn to her cozy condo/villa... yet, I was not the least bit interested in ever purchasing it.

While I was still at Linda's home, my husband stopped in for a 3-day visit, which changed the direction of our lives. Before we could understand what was happening, we found ourselves talking with my new-found friend about the possibility of our purchasing her place.

In the meantime, my heart was beginning to be inter-twined with Esther's story. Was the Lord prompting and moving us in this direction of a purchase? Was Australia soon to be added to my list of residences? I thought this surely couldn't be. This is so far beyond my "wildest imagination" that it wasn't even funny.

Well, I finished the book on Esther ... or perhaps I should rephrase that. The book "finished me." Both our lives were about to take an unbelievable turn that would surprise our socks off.

A NEW PLAN UNFOLDS

We told my new friend that we'd like to consider an offer and get back to her a week after arriving back in Canada. At least we would have a week of calm reflection to reconsider what seemed a completely unrealistic, and a ridiculous idea. Why would we even entertain the idea of moving "across such a large pond" to Australia?

Upon returning to Canada, we thought the distance from the friend and her Villa would change us, but after returning it seemed God was actively pursuing us for a wide change of events. To say the least, this was not in our itinerary of plans. We liked Australia, but move there?? NOT ON YOUR LIFE! ... or at least NOT IN *MY* LIFE, thank you.

But ... God had other plans. Over the next three months He introduced, arranged, rearranged and orchestrated an entirely new home for us. It would take many pages to unfold the many nuances of the story, but here a few highlights to encourage your heart and re-encourage myself.

God's GPS ... of Pain

It began as a resurgence of my almost crippling back pain within a few months after deciding to move to Australia. I was unable to stand for more than five minutes. Since many items had to be sold or disposed, I was beginning to feel like a "used car saleswoman." Photos and pricing for furniture and appliances were shared first with friends in emails, and then on a website.

I became a Downsizing Crusader, and sought a 90% reduction of our household. We had packed about 185 boxes, and the final count with wrapped items totaled 202! Every box was numbered and labelled on the outside with the entire contents of each box. What an undertaking. Also, all our belongings that were being shipped in a twenty-foot container were ready for loading in April [see photos].

One evening I awoke with the realization of all that was actually beginning to formulate and I immediately went into panic mode. I wasn't able to handle _anything_! And I mean anything including preparing meals. By now the pain in my back became increasingly unbearable. After reading my email, a friend phoned to ask what "medicine" I was taking to ease the pain. Just Tylenol, I confessed.

My personality allowed me to categorize and list dozens of reasons for anxiety. I needed to dwell on God's word as found in Philippians 2:13: "Cast all your cares upon Him, for He cares for you [and me]." Since I was unable to do anything else, all I could do was cast ... and cast I did.

I had a small lined booklet and began to fill six pages listing every item that caused me to "be concerned." Let's face it ... I WAS BECOMING SICK WITH WORRY! God prompted me to write them ALL down – naming them one by one (like the Hymn, 'Count Your Blessings ... Name Them One by One') ... and write I did.

But I was still in extreme pain. A therapist suggested I had a condition called Spinal Stenosis, and I needed to see a neurosurgeon as soon as possible. In the Canadian system you can either choose going through the public system to find a surgeon or pay privately. In my case, the wait list just to see a neurosurgeon was well over a year.

Through a series of events, both physically and financially, God provided the funds. I was able to have an MRI done within a week, and that was "miraculous." Once the results were issued, I phoned a surgical center in Canada and unbeknownst to me, I was given the name of the best neurosurgeon in Vancouver, Canada! My first consultation occurred within just a few days of my initial call, and eight days later I was on his table in surgery. THIS TRULY WAS MIRACULOUS in every sense of the word.

The months had rolled by quickly with downsizing, packing and emotionally shedding familiar furniture and surroundings. To this was added the pain and now surgery and healing. Through all this time, the Lord and I had many conversations, but it all boiled down to my need to LET GO.

After the surgery, all I could do for several days was either lie down, sit up for a little while or take tiny steps around the house, and soon, gingerly with much determination get up and walk down the street. Every time a "worrying thought or concern" would rise, all I could do was write it down and talk to the Lord. I was doing so much "casting," you would have thought I was an avid fisherman!

Our flight was booked to coincide with the arrival of the shipping container in Australia, our upcoming journey would occur within twelve days. Now, before we took our journey "across the pond" – a mere 7,397 miles (or 11,900 km), I still had no idea why God would move us there – even if for His purpose – not ours.

When we surrender to Jesus Christ, our loving, caring, and supremely trustful Savior, who orchestrates our lives and details the circumstances, asks us to move out of the known and comfortable into the unknown, the answer is yes…every time.

Perhaps in another story, I'll retell the fact that we can trust and rely on God for His good purpose. I'll close with the second verse of the hymn *"Praise to the Lord, The Almighty, The King of Creation"*:

> **"Hast thou not seen; all thy desires have been….**
> **granted in what He ordaineth."**

The move wasn't our idea – it was His, and there is no explanation for this move except the sovereignty of our God. And we are moving and trusting in one thing:

THE CHARACTER AND SOVEREIGNTY OF A LOVING AND SOVEREIGN GOD who has orchestrated it all!

May you be encouraged to walk with Him and trust Him in your life's daily activities and experience. He orchestrates our lives and steps to coincide with His wonderful purpose, in and through us, for others.

This photo won't mean anything to you, but to me, it represents "obedience" to the Lord.

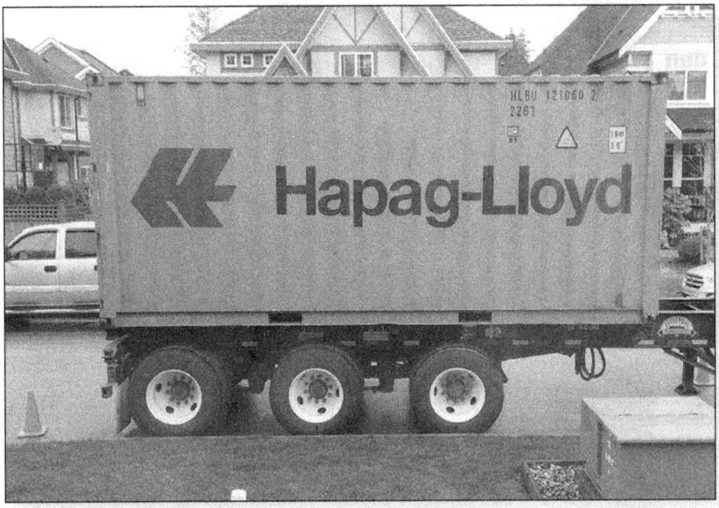
Hapag-Lloyd

What's That I See in Your Pantry?

We have all heard the phrase, "Little things mean a lot!" In this true kitchen adventure, "little things" should be likened to *"integrity in the pantry."* Let me start by introducing my pantry associate and on-site observer.

This event occurred one *ordinary morning* – at least I thought it was ordinary until the doorbell rang. I was surprised by a young ten-year-old friend standing at our front door. She was there to visit. I love pop-in guests because they catch us unprepared – you know … when we are being ourselves. They can then participate in whatever task we are undertaking.

Such surprises are also like an unplanned photo that captures us without makeup, and reveals our transparency … and goodness knows, we need more transparency in our relationships. Well, this one will surprise the socks right off of you.

Some of you might interpret "surprise at the front door" as a disruption. Whereas, God calls it a "divine interruption," and on this beautiful day, He was preparing me for a very sweet encounter.

Prior to the sound of the "doorbell", I was organizing our kitchen pantry. Imagine if you will, the kitchen counters full of all sorts of grocery items. Yes, my kitchen was an absolute mess.

In life, some of the most profound and meaningful lessons might occur when we are caught in the act of everyday living – whether our homes are tidy, or in a full-blown mess.

My little blonde-haired visitor could have cared less about my makeup, or the disarray on my kitchen counters. She came over to visit me! And what a joy she was!

What I love about children is that when they come to see you in your home, they're not coming for entertainment. They're coming over to just "be with you." After all, if my visitors are under three years of age, I just remove my Tupperware or pots and pans from a cupboard and they're happy for hours.

It didn't take rocket science to see that I was just cleaning the pantry and rearranging the items into a more logical layout. We chatted for some time about this and that, and all was well.

Then she asked for something to drink. Unprepared, I only had milk in the fridge … which wasn't one of her top five drink options. I responded with a "just milk." The odd thing about it was that she asked again, and I told her we didn't have any good carbonated beverages like a cola.

My response immediately created a coolness in the atmosphere, and I couldn't understand why the change in the emotional room temperature. Turning back toward the pantry, I knew instantly why she became so quiet.

On one of the shelves, she had seen a can of can of 7UP, and thought that would be an enjoyable treat. I am sure she assumed that I had lied to her about not having anything tasty to drink. Let me backtrack and explain, lest some of you think I'm a real jerk by keeping the soda to myself.

That can of 7UP was an empty security can in which you could place money or spare keys in. If anyone was around your home and looking for keys or money, they would never think of looking into a soda can.

As soon as I understood what was happening, I showed her the can and opened it. When the explanation was given, her sweet eyes became like giant marbles in disbelief. We both laughed hysterically.

It was a teachable moment for both of us. For things we see don't always appear as they really are. Yes, in life, many things are disguised to look appealing, yet in and of themselves they are empty.

It was important for her to know that I loved her, and would have shared anything in my cupboard with her. Also, my integrity was on the line, and the illustration of the 7UP was ideal.

Now, years later, this little one is a wonderful young mother with a family of her own, and we've grown very close over the years. We still look back at the day I was "honest" with her; and yes, *honesty is the best policy*. Had I not come clean about the "can in the pantry," she may never have trusted me with her heart and her friendship.

Life lessons are more often caught, than taught. Children learn from observing our lives. They're not looking for perfection, just "honesty."

Call me the next time you're tidying up your pantry and I'll bring the 7UP.

The Attentiveness of God

"Keepsakes of God to Treasure"

It's true – each day brings its own challenges. Very early one morning, my husband was to take an 8:00 a.m. flight, and we were on the road by 6:00 a.m. Thirty minutes later my husband stepped out of our car. He grabbed his luggage, kissed me goodbye and entered the airport. I got back into the car to drive home; but I was boxed in by cars in front of and beside me.

A few moments later the car next to me pulled away. Yes! Here was my opportunity to pull away from the curb and begin the drive home. Even though the space was clear, and my foot was firmly on the brake, I double-checked over my shoulder for any additional cars. Once certain that all was clear, I placed my foot on the accelerator and I was *off*.

The *all clear* I had just confirmed, suddenly changed in a matter of seconds. The next thing I remember was a huge noise, sudden darkness, and a blast that felt like a bombshell coming toward me, and an explosion in my face.

I should pause here for a moment, because I find the retelling of this incident somewhat difficult.

I was immediately *stunned*, followed in quick succession by shock, blurred vision, and nausea. It took a few seconds to realize that the car I was driving had plowed into something extremely hard. A CEMENT GUARD WALL is what they call it.

Thinking smoke was filtering in the air, I needed to exit the car. I later found out that these were particles from the now-deployed airbag which filled the car. I was also amazed that the car door was partially opened, due to the impact into the wall. Thankfully it was open enough that I could sort of crawl out the bottom half of the door, as the upper half was consumed with the air bag.

Our little Papillon dog was in the seat next to me. She had been thrown into the glove compartment area and thankfully only suffered a slight cut on her head. I placed the leash around her neck, picked up my dog, grabbed my purse and crawled out of the car.

After exiting the car, the first order of business was to hold onto my little dog and purse and cross three lanes of airport traffic. Gosh those airbags take up a lot of space when they "explode in front of you!"

I was quite nauseous and my vision was blurred. I knew I had to get into the airport and tell someone I needed help. I raised my arm and began waving at the cars so they would see me and stop to allow me to cross the traffic lanes. The car was demolished, and need for help was increasing. Thinking back, I would never have attempted any of that in a thousand years!

No one was approaching the car to help me. But there was One who was there all the time and proved Himself "faithful" in incredible ways. This included crossing three lanes of oncoming traffic while disoriented, as I needed to get inside the airport, where I called out to the first man I saw and exclaimed that I had been in an accident, was sick and couldn't see straight; and that I needed to lie down *right away*.

I needed help and quickly. Dizzy and unstable on my feet, I managed to make my way to some seats still cradling our little dog. I phoned my husband, who was well past security, and in the secure waiting area preparing to board his flight. No answer! His phone must have been turned off, so I sent a text. I phoned two other people, but since it was 6:40 a.m., their phones must have been off as well.

Just before the pain struck, my cell phone rang. It was my husband, "Are you all right, and where are you?" "I'm at the airport – I haven't gone anywhere." *Gone nowhere ... really?*

At this point, I could not function. With my coat under my head, I laid down on the seat, and our little dog curled up on my tummy. My blurred vision cleared, but pain was beginning to settle in my back and neck. I could only quietly say, "Jesus, help me."

In what seemed like a couple of minutes, the area around me was flooded with "visitors." My husband, Peter, was escorted back through Security to where I was located – though horizontal. The crowd consisted of four policemen, six paramedics, a fire truck, emergency squad and a tow truck driver. Goodness, a person has to go through quite an ordeal to locate a group of *personal followers.*

Sounds humorous, but it wasn't funny at the time! One paramedic was telling me that I needed to be taken to the hospital; but I told him that I wasn't going anywhere until my little pooch (Puppet) was taken care of. The wonderful paramedic not only read the situation medically, but emotionally.

He leaned over me and said, "We're not taking you anywhere until your little Puppet has been taken care of." Aww, how tenderly his words were spoken, and at least one worry was put to rest.

Peter took the dog and gave her to our friend (who had by now arrived at the airport) along with the keys to the house, and asked for the dog to be taken to our home and locked the house.

The pain was setting in, and I was now happy to be transported to a hospital. Not so fast! A policeman wanted to do an interview! He was asking me about the details of what had just happened. I don't mind being questioned, but would have preferred a slightly more convenient time, and in a relaxed atmosphere.

There was nothing my husband could do, as he was already checked in and waiting to board an aircraft. He walked alongside me as they transported me into the ambulance; and I assured him that he could do nothing to help me, but to go ahead on his trip.

I don't remember much more, except that I was in an *emergency vehicle* and I was scared, yet felt safe because the paramedics know how to care for you. If you've been in one, you probably know the feeling.

Well, my "personal paramedic" was sent by the Lord! He gently checked for symptoms of perhaps a broken neck, etc. Once convinced that my neck wasn't fractured, he leaned over me and asked, "Dianne, are you a Christian?" "Yes, I am" was my response. He then said, "I am too, and honey we're going to take *real good care* of **you**!" I almost cried at his tender and compassionate response.

I knew then, that God was indeed present and caring for me in such kind and wonderful ways.

To breathe in some fresh air on this accident, I'd like to leave the *cement situation* behind me, and invite you to the many *attentive ways* my Savior supported me in the trauma of the event.

First, my husband would normally not be allowed out of the pre-boarding waiting area to return through the security check area of the airport. This typically one-way process essentially seals him in for his flight.

The airport staff made an exception and escorted him to my *horizontal location*. It's at this point that I realized God made sure I could see my husband before heading toward the hospital. That would give both of us a sense of peace.

Here's another incredible thing God did for me: I wasn't fearful of being left alone, but encouraged my husband to continue on with his needed travel plans. Are you kidding? As I review it again, that wasn't a "normal response" of a wife who was in my condition at the moment. It was as if God "took over" my responses and gave me PEACE ... an INCREDIBLE PEACE.

A few days before my husband's trip away and a rude introduction to a wall, I kept sharing with the Lord that I had no *projects* at home to do. My housework was caught up (which seldom happens), and there were no laundry or painting plans. What was I going to do for seven days? While being examined in the ambulance, a humorous thought came my way. It was as though the Lord said, "I have an idea what you'll do: REST." I could only smile ... since laughter was not possible.

Another incredible thing God did for me: I wasn't one bit afraid! Sure, I was hurting, but I had "no stress." I'm amazed I'm even writing this down, but it's true. I was now *alone* in an ambulance heading to an unknown destination for who knows how long. My husband had returned to the pre-boarding area, and a friend had taken my dog home.

Yet another incredible thing God provided for me: The emergency room wasn't busy! I was taken to an empty area – you know, the ones where a baby blue curtain separated you from your hospital neighbor. Within minutes I was surrounded by two nurses and a physician and my *personal paramedic*, Ray. The nurse was on-the-spot with the needle for one arm in case I required blood.

God helped with another incredible thing: Standing to my right, the paramedic and physician were chatting about my "high blood pressure." In defense of my *medical rights*, I piped up and said: "Hey, your blood pressure would be high too if you just slammed into a cement wall like I did." I began to laugh, and they did too. "Just patch me up and get me out of here and my *white coat syndrome* will reduce to a normal range."

Here's another incredible way God showed up: Within half an hour, my entire head was placed in a cage. They weren't lying when they told me it would be uncomfortable! Even as they fitted this gear on me, *the Lord calmed my mind and heart with a promise to be still and you'll be safe.*

I wasn't allowed to move, but I'd be safe. Now the ceiling was my new panoramic view. God provided a brief, wonderful presence through a nurse who juggled her time between me and new ER patients. Though by myself, I was not alone – God was with me. Within just a few minutes, I heard the familiar voice of a friend.

This friend had been told of my situation, and had come to the hospital to *be with me.* She announced firmly that she would be there all the time so I wouldn't be alone. In addition, she would drive me home after the tests were complete and I was discharged. This was truly another provision of the Lord Jesus, and though He was there, He wanted me *to experience "Jesus with skin on"– through my friend's physical presence to further comfort me.* I was stunned, and wanted to leap for joy when I heard my friend's voice. However, due to the attached apparatus, I was prevented from any actual leaping.

Here's another incredible way God showed up: My personal *paramedic* reappeared at the hospital, likely with another patient. Lying on my back, I could see people coming and going. I called out, "There's Ray … my paramedic," and he instantly came over to my palatial, though temporary accommodation. I thanked and encouraged him because of the way he had attended to me earlier that morning.

Right then and there, I planned to write him a letter, to not only thank him, but to encourage him in how good he is at his job (actually *his ministry* to others). *Perhaps this was one of the purposes in all of the events – a paramedic needed encouragement.*

Within two hours, testing was complete, and with no broken bones, I was released within the next hour.

Here's another incredible way God cared for me: My friend drove me home and stayed with me the entire day and evening just to make sure I would be all right staying by myself. The pain medicine was to be my regular companion for a few months, but for today she wasn't going to leave me until I felt comfortable being alone.

The following three evenings she came over to attend to me with hour long massages. What a *gift* she was. She even brought home three meals since I was too weak to prepare anything for myself.

Here's other way God provided for me: Two of my neighbors also came over with food on various days, while another neighbor brought flowers.

I have mused over God's intervention through this ordeal: Here a few entries from my journal as reminders of God's provision and faithfulness:

Mental gifts from my Lord ... through and because of the accident:

- I can attest that all this has given me a "deeper and more intimate" walk with Jesus
- There are purposes in our trials (and I've only seen just a few)
- Adjusting to God's plan B ... develops my character
- Giving of ourselves in those moments of pain, we'll have **"keepsakes of Him to treasure"**

A *keepsake* is something precious that serves as a reminder, a memorial or symbol of a treasure to our hearts. I wanted to write about this event in my journal and treasure these *keepsakes* of Jesus and His marvelous care in all that transpired."

Before I close off this personal story, I want to share the Scripture that I was memorizing just weeks before the incident at the airport.

> Psalm 28:7 "The Lord is my *strength* and my *shield*; my heart trusted in Him, and I am helped."

That verse came to me soon after the accident reminding me of His constant care in and through everything, and I couldn't be more GRATEFUL!!! Every word of that verse was lived out that morning, and continues to remain as I heal.

As people ask me about what happened that day, I want to be keenly aware that even if I shared the details, the most important details were "about God ... and how He came near to attend me in every way."

We have, or will experience disappointment, pain, frustration, and various forms of grief woven throughout life, because we live in a sinful world. It's easy to camp on the negative as we tell our stories, but we need to be confident to share what "God does" for His people in the midst of our life experiences. Why? To give hope to others – through which they are encouraged to trust Him in their life journey.

At the time of this writing, it has been three and a half months since this event ... and though I am not fully recovered, I still recall it all with a "grateful heart."

Since driving (and living) has its own dangers, we can nevertheless tell others of our experiences – good and bad – and add a *BUT GOD* component because of what He does to care and provide for us.

When we tell others of how God helps us, it should *highlight* our experience of His presence and help. Telling others of our daily walk with Jesus enforces the worth and worthiness of our complete trust in Him while we walk here on earth ... and right on into eternity.

Just One Amongst the Crowd

When you're around a group of people, do you sometimes feel as if you're just "one" amongst the crowd? Though I'm not interested in drawing a crowd, but the "little girl" in me wonders if anyone notices my coming and going. For example, when moving through crowd exiting a church, I think to myself, I wonder, *"Does anyone notice me?"* Have you ever thought about that for yourself?

Several years ago, I came across some verses in the book of Luke that were like a megaphone. May I take a few minutes to encourage you as the Lord allowed me insight from a man of small-stature in the crowd?

We have all been given **the look** by someone. You know, some non-verbal communication indicating you had lipstick on your front teeth, or broccoli between them, or a spouse indicating it's time to go "home." Luke 19:5 embraces "a look" that changed everything!

"And when Jesus came to the place, He looked up at Zacchaeus and called him by name." Jesus gave a personal, facial invitation to a small-statured man nestled in a tree. In this verse, I was drawn to the words." He looked."

We've all been there ... listening to someone, or so taken up with the moment, we lost sight of everyone around us. Zacchaeus was in this zone.

These words have been simmering in my heart and mind, and have given me encouragement in my walk with the Lord, as well as the motivation to mentor other women.

The first thing I noticed is that <u>Jesus stopped</u>. Though He was on assignment, and there were crowds of people, Jesus stopped and turned to look at *one man*, Zacchaeus who was curious about Jesus.

Jesus knew this man inside out – He knew his heart, his mind, and all that was going on in his life...just as He knows about your life and mine. Jesus knew that within this little man who climbed a tree just to "look" at Him was a deep-seeded curiosity.

Jesus understood what Zacchaeus' inner desire was. It is likely that Zacchaeus was unaware. You and I know people working and living around us who are just like Zacchaeus. They are oblivious to the hollowness in their souls, or of their need of Christ.

For Zacchaeus the tree was how he could get a better look. He did not climb up to draw attention to himself. He just wanted somewhere to see this Teacher whom he had heard so much about. In essence Jesus' reputation of being *winsome* had attracted Zacchaeus to go to such trouble.

God had directed the intersection in the lives of Jesus and Zacchaeus (in this crowd). In the same way, God directs our steps which are "ordained of the Lord."

Jesus teaches us about His deep care and concern for someone written off by others. His look rightly assessed the need in Zacchaeus' heart, and Jesus took the extra step of publicly saying that He would eat with him. When their eyes met – their relationship began, and Zacchaeus was never the same.

A further examination of Jesus' look yields three characteristics:

First, it was **PERSONAL**: Jesus noticed *one particular individual* in the middle of a throng of people. Jesus found him because He knew exactly where he was, and wanted to relate to him *one-on-one*.

From the look, Zacchaeus knew he wasn't just one of the crowd, but someone who was loved, and cared for. Consider how today it is easy to get lost in social media's continual waterfall of "data." It is easy to overlook someone who might be seeking. Remember that in Psalm 37:23 we read how the Lord *delights in every detail of our lives.*

Second, His look was **PERSUASIVE**: Jesus invited Himself over to the man's home for dinner as His plan was for a relationship that would last forever. This look and subsequent action brought about personal repentance and change in Zacchaeus. Why? Jesus saw an opportunity to connect in that moment.

For most of us, our lives are much like "oatmeal" or "vanilla" with no major events that would distinguish us from thousands of others. However, in our everyday living, we have "Divine appointments" which God has prepared beforehand … just waiting for our participation through a smile, hug, call, text, or email. This is like our look toward an individual, who, like Zacchaeus, is waiting to be noticed. Could it be the mailman, garbage collector, salesperson, or a person passing on the street? Let's keep our eyes open for people in the trees.

Third, His look was **PERMANENT**: Zacchaeus' life was changed forever … never the same again. He became a *"new man"* because of the way in which Jesus *"looked"* at him. This is the message we need to understand and tell others … Jesus is looking toward them.

Herein is this great truth. Jesus wants to have fellowship with each one of us. The practical application is that God chooses to use us to be His servants, who, when placed in a situation, will allow us to connect as He brings others along our pathway of our life.

Perhaps some have walked "with us" for a season, and have helped show us Christ's love. It is our turn to be ready, willing, and able to do the same for others. Let's see how these truths might look in the shoe leather of our lives?

May the Lord adjust the *lens of our eyes* to look at others the way He does.

New Soil for a New Season

As a preface to this story, I have to admit that there is a Gardener in my heart and soul Who has stirred my often-stagnant heart to confess that truth. These often-dormant potions of my heart aren't very large, but they are tiny spots that occasionally miss the Son's touch of refreshment and life-giving encouragement.

With full disclosure, I must say that I didn't even realize that the soil of my heart had become secluded and malnourished, because I was afraid of traversing the landscape of grief. This grief wasn't due to someone leaving this life. Rather, there was a sense that the soil of my life had been altered, and that the roots of my existence no longer found nourishment.

This deep upheaval stirring within me makes this difficult to write, but there is no other outlet. It's as though a passion growing deep inside my heart could not find any means of outward expression.

This is one of those few things in life where talking to a few close friends does not provide an answer, nor was there relief in speaking with my husband. However, since I know the Lord understands and cares, it is only He who can provide the "nutrient of grace." This dependence on Him brings me peace knowing that His sovereignty rules over all.

Sovereignty is defined as: supreme authority, control, and power, over all that has happened, is happening, and will happen, in all times, and across all history; and to govern all that happens, and what has, is, or will happen, will always be in accordance to His Divine will.

There is great comfort knowing that God alone has the right to achieve His purpose, and has the power to bring about circumstances that dictate whatever He wills to come to pass. He has complete control over everything, and there is nothing that is done that is not done or allowed according to His will.

> Proverbs 16:6 "The heart of man plans his way, but the Lord establishes his steps."

> Zechariah 4:6 "This is the word of the Lord to Zerubbabel: Not by might, nor by power, but by my Spirit, says the Lord of hosts."

> Psalm 103:19, "The Lord has established His throne in heaven, and His kingdom rules over all."

Viewing these verses, I am reminded that I am not in charge of any "opportunities for ministry," God is. There have been several occasions when I've been introduced to a few relationships, and begin to sense that God is at work in that moment. It is then, I'm transplanted again out of that situation and into the home of my garden.

A beautiful garden brings such joy and beauty to me. It is like when I meet other women, and see their world as their garden of beauty, and I want to be involved in the soil of their lives. After a few meaningful conversations, my heart begins to beat with the expectation of where this relationship might be headed.

In the past, I could sense when the gates of these gardens would close, and I'd return home with disappointment flooding my heart and mind.

Now, seeing my thoughts on paper has helped me realize, that I'm not the one responsible for my life, my opportunities, my purpose, my fulfillment. God is the One in the driver's seat. Of course, buried just below the surface of my actions is pride. Yes, I want my life to count for eternity, and I long to come alongside other women and share truths and experiences from my walk with Him. Don't you share my desire?

Living a Compelling Life

One of my pastimes is cruising through a dictionary or thesaurus. Thankfully I don't need permission or a driver's license for these "word tours", and they do give direction to the use of words.

I am surprised when I locate a particular word–thinking I already know the meaning, but have frequently been way off course.

So, before we delve into the characteristics of a compelling lifestyle, let's navigate through some descriptions of the word "compelling."

Webster's dictionary helps, and starts us on the trail of discovering some of the depth of the word "compelling."

First the definition: Evoking interest or admiration in a powerfully irresistible way, captivating, irresistible, inspiring, convincing, believable, persuasive, potent, credible, efficacious, reasonable, telling, conclusive, unanswerable, influential.

As well a verse from 2 Corinthians 5:20–"We are therefore Christ's ambassadors, as though God were making his appeal through us. We implore you on Christ's behalf: Be reconciled to God."

The verse should provoke every person who is a follower of Christ to seek to be the best ambassador he or she can be.

An ambassador is sent by a head of state, and represents their home country, its culture, lifestyle, and priorities in a foreign land.

We are God's ambassador and all that He represents. Though we are far from perfect, God uses us and assigns each of us an "area of influence."

I have often heard believers say they yearn to be God's witnesses on earth.

What makes me chuckle is that we don't have to "try" to be God's emissaries, we already "are."

The way we act, speak, listen, care, love and respond to people "is our witness." Our interactions with others enable others to see who is our "Head of State" – the Lord Jesus. After seeing us, people can say to themselves, "This person represents Jesus Christ!"

Before we shudder in our flip flops or runners, let's review that concept again. Clearly expressed, it means that people look at our lives and form an "opinion about Jesus Christ" after they've watched, listened, worked, and lived next to us.

Before leaving this topic, I should add that if you feel convicted, get in line behind me! Aren't we grateful that we're all "in process" of becoming more like Jesus. I do hope this is "your personal goal." We need to see more people more like Jesus in our world.

In practice, one wonders if anyone heard the stirring sermon on being more like Jesus when we see the antics of cars leaving the church parking lot, and drivers forgetting to display patience and courtesy in their exit.

I've seen people walk out the church door like a saint, and drive like a *<pause> maniac* who hasn't taken their medication.

The following story is about a friend and mentor who moved "home with Jesus," but her character traits have remained with me.

A beautiful truth is that we become like the people we spend the most time with. That has merit in many arenas.

I observed the beauty of my dear friend's behavior in myriads of circumstances, and which have become life lessons. She left me a "living legacy ... to live up to."

Actually, we all leave a legacy. How we live, love, and serve others determines its accuracy in being "more like Jesus."

My friend demonstrated what it means to live a compelling life; a life that points to our living Savior, Jesus Christ.

Jesus was compelled to go to the cross for each one of us, and took on Himself the death penalty our sins deserved. He willingly laid down His life so we would know how much He loves us, and wants us with Him for eternity.

We have all probably seen someone who was saved from a devastating or life-threatening accident; and when they meet their rescuer they exclaim with enthusiastic praise, "I can't thank you enough; I owe you my life."

The person rescued cannot express their gratitude enough. In order to be a promoter of the Lord Jesus Christ, we need observable character traits that direct others towards Him.

My mentor and friend left these legacies for me to ruminate in my heart and mind. I can almost hear her say, "If I had only lived better and been more honoring to Jesus." She quietly mentored my heart and life in many ways.

The essence of her life spoke loud and clear to me. She communicated through her tone, or silence as the situation demanded, and always expressed herself with grace. She had the most remarkable way of "swallowing her words" before they exited her lips.

She never spoke glowingly about herself; but she always seemed to blossom with kindness, compassion, and gentleness when speaking about others. No wonder I loved being around her.

She always saw my "potential" instead of the poverty of my behavior. Her nature gravitated toward showing me a better way ... Jesus' way of handling others.

My friend would *"re-frame* situations" to observe, react and redirect any negativity she faced into a Jesus-like response. I learned by "watching her."

We can listen to a sermon on Sunday or at any other time on the internet, but I'd rather *"observe one"* first hand anytime.

Godly character is beautiful to behold and walk alongside in any relationship. Our lives influence others, even when we're not aware of it. I was privileged to write a tribute about my friend, because her life was a compelling tribute to God.

And oh, how I desire to live in such a way that people will want to know and fall in love with Jesus.

The Bible – God's Word, is our navigational tool and our compass. It provides illumination, direction, opportunity, intervals, character, and instruction, so that we can live life to its finest.

A compass question for all of us to answer is this: **"What do people think about God after spending time with you or with me? Does anything else in life really matter?"**

What is Your Calling? What is Your Passion?

What breathes air into your lungs? What gives you inner joy?

As I begin to wind down the retelling of my stories, or as I refer to them, *my encounters with the Living God,* my prayer has been that your heart has been stirred, and your life energized to begin a journey with Jesus of your own.

When I began my journey with God years ago, I never realized that God's design was for people to know Him, enjoy Him, and journey through life with Him. Back then, I used to feel God was abstract and incapable of knowing. Sadly, I discovered that I was just living a *religion*, not experiencing a *relationship*.

I hope you can understand my passion, because it is my delight to know that God wants to be in a *personal relationship with me*, daily. However, Jesus is a gentleman, and He will never push His way into a life. He wants us to recognize our need for Him.

The need begins with our understanding that He is Holy, and we are not………… and that our sin and waywardness need to be dealt with.

God dealt with it all right by providing a loving substitute – His Son – to come and take the punishment for our sins upon Himself through dying on a cross, and making a way for us to be restored to a loving relationship with God.

That is the "good news!" Jesus came here to earth to show us what God the Father is like. ***Jesus is God ... with skin on.*** He died the death our sin deserves, and the offer of His righteousness (or perfection) awaits us. However, this offer is like a GIFT that has to be received ... personally.

In John 14:6 we read: "Jesus answered, "I am the way and the truth and the life. No one comes to the Father except through Me."

Not long ago I wondered, "How will I wrap up these stories?" I carefully use *wrap up* and not *end*, because each day of living offers opportunities to see God at work in our lives. There is a thrill that occurs when we respond to God's promptings in our life. He is involved in our circumstances, and enables us to see our waywardness and desire to be opposed to Him. Once we understand and admit our condition, and request God's presence and leadership in our lives, we are finally able to perceive Him spiritually.

Here are a few thoughts from the book of Ephesians: Ephesians 1:18: "I pray that the eyes of your heart may be enlightened in order that you may know **the hope to which He has called you...**"

Ephesians 2:10 states: "For we are God's handiwork (masterpiece), created in Christ Jesus to do good works, which **God prepared in advance for us to do.**"

Perhaps like me, you are thinking: "What is my calling?" and, "What has God asked me to do?"

These are sobering thoughts which clarified a few things for me. First, like you, I want to receive a "well done" from Him which I hope to receive by being faithful to what He has asked me to do. Second, I will never be compared to anyone else.

So, my heart sprang into a prayer: *Father, help me RECOGNIZE what You are asking me to do each day, and please give me the strength and wisdom to do what You ask.*

Since He will not ask the results of things that He didn't ask me to do (such as my personal plans and ideas). The question then is simple enough: "Did I do each day what was asked of me?"

Luke 16:10 "One who is faithful in a very little is also faithful in much...."

- What is **my** calling? What has God asked **me** to do?
- What is **your** calling? What has God asked **you** to do?

NOTE: There are no earth-shaking tasks placed before us. Our "well done" is based on the tasks given to us – usually ... the little things ... the everyday, ordinary, insignificant things of life.

Who knew God likes oatmeal? Each day is an opportunity for God to express Himself in and through each of us in such simple, insignificant, oatmeal-kind-of-ordinary ways. God is extraordinary in using ordinary people in ordinary circumstances. Thus, God's intervention can occur in the extra-large or extra-small situations, or in moments that are incredibly meaningful or just plain macaroni.

Have you had a personal encounter with God? Why not stop right now and extend an invitation for Him to come into your life, forgive all your sins, and begin a journey through your life. A journey you neither imagined or thought possible. Remember, He has plans far greater than you could ever conceive.

It is with this in mind, I began writing my stories ... which are really His stories of how He came near to show me that *He is real and yearns to be involved in the details of my life ... and in yours as well.*

> "But God chose the foolish things of the world to shame the wise; God chose the weak things of the world to shame the strong." 1 Corinthians 1:27

I close with the following thought:

Jesus is EXTRAORDINARY amongst the ORDINARY!

And I love that about Him, don't you? We don't have to do big things, just little things with a big heart for Him. He turns the *mundane* into **magnificent** and the *ordinary* into **extraordinary!**"

Oh, that our lives are lived in such a way that produces a "yearning for God" in others.

What apparent foolish and insignificant things are you involved in for the Kingdom of God and His glory?

In Honor of *Your* Birthday

My husband and I have been privileged to meet so many lovely people. We have friends from age 3 to 103. I have learned, listened, and loved all of them for a variety of reasons. Some are single, some are married, some are divorced, some are widows and widowers.

Each one is precious, and God has allowed our paths not only to cross, but intertwine. I've been richer for the treasure they have brought to my life. Some are here on earth while others are rejoicing with Jesus.

One such friend who is now in the presence of the Lord, brought so much richness of laughter and the beautiful qualities of a Godly character into our lives. We had known this man for several years, and prior to our friendship, he had been married to his sweetheart for many years. Whenever the conversation turned to her, his face would light up with delight. Now, as a widower, he was learning to walk alone without her.

In spite of his "experience," he maintained a tender disposition and childlike joy. He was the type of person with whom you could discuss "oatmeal" and be bursting at the seams with laughter about its consistency. We would laugh about almost anything. Together we often saw the funny side of things.

One day, while at our home for morning tea, we discovered that he had a birthday coming up. It would be the celebration of 80 wonderful years. My mind soon went into high gear, and I began planning a birthday dinner party in his honor. We had phoned our friend to invite him and his new "significant other" lady friend for dinner. That was the plan, at least that's what he thought. He did not know, we also informed eight friends of the upcoming event.

He was turning 80 and had no need of gifts. But the Lord brought to my mind that there was one gift that would be especially appropriate. That gift was ENCOURAGEMENT.

Now how do you wrap and present a gift like that? I'd been to many birthday parties and they all consisted of food, gifts and an occasional balloon. It took a few days for me to think through this surprise party, and how we all could encourage him.

If you're anything like me, when someone compliments or makes an encouraging comment to me, I cannot remember one of those encouraging words after five seconds. Oh, I wish I could, but it seems that all the goodness of the positive comment said are scattered to the four winds.

Then it came to me! If we each purchased a card and wrote all the wonderful things we'd like to say to him, ways he had encouraged us and how he built positive qualities into our life as well as the things we've appreciated and loved about him ... it seemed like a wonderful and creative way to show our love for him.

When I phoned each of his friends, I told them of the idea of a BIRTHDAY "encouragement" PARTY. They all readily agreed. The plan was that our friend would come over for dinner, and about 45 minutes later, his friends would keep showing up at the front door.

They were to bring their "written gift," and later, after cake and ice cream, each of us were going to "read aloud" our card to him. I even had a tape recorder ready for the occasion in the background.

The evening was filled with surprises, laughter and tears–tears of joy and appreciation. I doubt that any of us would forget that evening. I know our guest of honor wouldn't as we gifted him with a tape of the party, and the recording of each of his friends' comments of appreciation for his life.

The following morning our "Birthday Celebrant" phoned to tell me that this 80th birthday party was the first birthday party he had ever had in "his honor;" and he remarked that it was the most meaningful evening of his life.

I learned something very important from this event—that regardless of our age, we all need to know that we're special … special to someone. Perhaps you've never received this kind of personal encouragement. Unfortunately, it seems that funerals are when many speak glowingly of the value of the deceased. The sad part is, the one who needed to hear that encouragement from others is no longer able to hear it.

I know many of us weren't raised receiving any regular verbal comments like, "I love you"; "You're special to me"; and "You've enriched my life in many ways," and so on. For some it's our upbringing within a social or ethnic environment where such things would often be frowned upon. Thus, there is rarely a verbal expression of love or affirmation.

Remember, each day is precious! Every time you meet with a friend or chat with them on the phone is a moment that can never be repeated.

Through some precious experiences over the last 20 years, I have learned the value and joy of telling others that I love them. Often at the end of every conversation with those I love, I tell them plainly, "I love you" without being mushy, or dripping all over them.

Each day is a GIFT…that's why it is called the PRESENT.

Consider "gifting others" with our verbal encouragement on a regular basis.

Gardening in my Heels

Have you ever taken a quick look at someone and made an assumption ... without having all the facts? Unfortunately, this is true of someone who looks at you as well. This incident took place years ago, and I still laugh at how assumptions can lead us astray.

One morning a friend and I were getting ready to drive to a conference. Arrangements were made that she would drive over to pick me up at a certain time. This event called for wearing something a little dressy. My bathroom mirror was a bit too truthful that morning, so I was making the necessary adjustments as needed. I primped and prodded ... working carefully and craftily for a respectable public appearance. I even decided to wear heels.

I surprised myself by being ready 15 minutes ahead of my friend's scheduled arrival, and wondered what little task I could busy myself with while waiting. I stepped outside, and noticed that the weeds in our front garden needed attention. I pulled out the spade from the garage and set off to attend to the errant weeds. Of course, those weeds can go down deep, so I used the spade to cut down to the roots.

This task would have been much easier if I was wearing my normal gardening attire, loose clothing and tennis shoes. However, it was more of a challenge in my dress and high heels. No matter, and since I was determined, I carried on. I checked every now and then to see if my friend had arrived

Time passed, and I was making real progress, even in heels. I was practically finished, when my friend pulled into the driveway. She looked at me oddly as I approached her car. We both broke out laughing when she told me she had never seen anyone garden in heels. Of course, I explained that I was simply trying to use my time wisely while waiting for her to arrive, and we laughed again.

Days passed, and it was Sunday morning. The worship service was over and several of us were gathered in the foyer talking. A woman approached me with an odd look on her face. She asked me if I garden in heels. My response was no, and I just laughed. But another odd expression came over her face as she started to explain that she just happened to be driving past our home that week and she thought she saw me in heels digging in my garden.

I burst out laughing, desperately trying to re-align her assumptions about my choice of gardening attire. After I shared "why" I was wearing heels, she too broke out laughing.

Her first comment to herself was that she assumed that she and I could never be friends because she thought I was odd and assumed I always gardened in heels.

We both have had many laughs about the incorrect assumption she had simply because she didn't have all the facts. I asked her if I could use that illustration while teaching in a Bible Study to highlight how easily we can misjudge a person when we don't have all the details of the situation. She agreed and I have used that story as it continues to be a reminder to me to not make a quick assumption or worse, a rash judgement about anyone, even if they are doing something quite odd and out of the ordinary.

... and .... No! I have never worn heels in the garden since!

A Lingering Fragrance

Like most of us, our days are "very ordinary." Our respective journeys through life are more like sleepy bus rides rather than a long string of adrenaline pumping action sequences. It would be rare, very rare indeed, if we were to receive a phone call from the local newspaper or TV channel requesting an interview about some dramatic highlight that had occurred within the walls of our home. I don't think I have ever heard of *vacuuming and laundry* as lead stories for the evening news. We just live out our *very ordinary* days in sequence, don't we?

I often think about and appreciate that, "God is often at work making the ordinary into the *extraordinary* in our lives" to fulfill His purpose, as well as in the lives of others".

The most recent neighborhood we lived in had a transcendent beauty with an ever-changing panorama that transformed with the season. When we purchased our home, it had been sorely neglected for several years, and desperately needed a complete overhaul both inside and out. And so we began the work.

I tackled most of the landscaping, and as a result, I got to know most of the people living around us. Almost every inch of the yard needed to be tackled, and I often pondered, "Why Lord?" Meanwhile, I dug, chopped, weeded, mowed, and watered, and people would stop to view the progress and see how I was doing. I came to realize that as neighbors walked their dogs, or jogged by daily, my visibility and availability became a purposeful method the Lord laid before me to be a cheerful witness for Him.

Late one afternoon, the doorbell rang, and it was one of those neighbors who would periodically stop by to talk while I worked. She stood there clutching a dish of lasagna for me with both hands. What a delightful surprise!

This was lovely on two counts: First, I didn't have to prepare it, and second, lasagna is one of my favorites. If you know anything about lasagna, you know that the perfume of garlic permeates the kitchen. Mumm! What an aroma when you're hungry.

Of course, I invited her inside for a little chat, and she followed me into the kitchen. I placed her thoughtful delivery on the counter for our dinner that night. In the past, conversation with this woman was never difficult. She is one of those persons who knew not only how to listen, but how to keep a conversation interesting and alive.

It wasn't long however before she said she needed to get back to her home so that she could finish preparing dinner for her family. She sauntered to the front door, and gave me a big hug in parting.

So, what was so special about all of this? Yes, the dinner she brought was both thoughtful and kind, but there was something else that occurred as a result of her visit that left a lasting impression. What was it?

After bidding her farewell, I entered my home and closed the door. I was greeted with a distinct and fragrant aroma in our house. Was it the smell of the garlic in the lasagna? No! It was the lingering scent of the cologne she had been wearing. Her beautiful perfume wafted in the air. It wasn't just at the entrance, but it had permeated through the living room, and all the way into the kitchen, remaining in the atmosphere for more than an hour.

As I was pondering that, the Lord brought to my mind, the Scripture:

> 2 Corinthians 2:14-16 "For we are to God, the fragrance of Christ."

My neighbor's presence lingered long after she had gone from our house, because she had "adorned herself" with perfume earlier in the day which was still emanating from her permeating the air in our home.

Yes, Lord, I see! That's the effect our Savior longs for us as to have as we interact and rub shoulders others. Wherever we are, whatever we do, we are to emanate the "fragrant love of Christ."

I laugh when I think of consuming garlic which does not remain a secret, because it just emits from your pores. So, in a spiritual sense, we shouldn't need to advertise that we've had our *quiet time* or have read the Bible that day because others should witness the evidence of Christ in our lives and sense the presence of His love.

The presence and residence of the Holy Spirit within every believer should be the "aroma and the character of Christ" radiating from our life. There ought to be something about us that attracts people to the character of Jesus Christ within us.

It calls for "contagious Christian living!"

> Acts 4:13 "When they saw the courage of Peter and John and realized that they were unschooled, ordinary men, they were astonished and they took note that these men had been with Jesus."

If we have learned anything from our recent Global Pandemic, we know that we cannot infect someone by just *talking about it* – we must be infected in order to infect or affect someone else. In other words, we ourselves must be CONTAGIOUS.

In reality, as followers of Jesus Christ, His nature, character, and teaching should exude from the pores of our lives! So that when others spend time with us, they'll be affected – even in a tiny way – by the love of God.

I have shared this concept in other stories, but it bears repeating. When people observe us, what do they think? When they listen to our talk *about others*; work alongside us; see our response to criticism or negative circumstances; observe our work ethic; or evaluate our integrity and authenticity, what do they think?

God can take how we live and treat others and make an impression upon the life, heart, and soul of another. That makes the ordinary extraordinary. Could we make for ourselves a life goal which begins by asking?

> "After people spend time with us, what do they think of Jesus?"

We are always making an impression! What is it? What fragrance of Christ and His character and love do we leave?

This spiritual aroma, resulting from our encounter with Christ, blesses the heart of God. The Father loves to see the life of His Son being "expressed" in and through our daily living. May the Lord help each of us leave a lasting and loving fragrance of Jesus Christ though our words and lifestyle into every relational encounter, for His glory!

Tea For Two

This little tea party took place in Southern California. We had moved from Washington State to Ventura, California. Everything was new again: a new home, a new neighborhood, and a new church. I've moved enough to know that those first few months in a new location can bring on some depression and sadness.

Most of this can be quite normal when you've been uprooted from one home to another, and for a time you can be emotionally "fragile."

My husband went off to work, and as I looked around at the collage of boxes waiting to be opened, I felt overwhelmed. For me, that's the time to put first things first. It's time to pull away, grab my Bible and a cup of tea, and have a mini retreat. Goodness knows I had a wide variety of things to chat over with Jesus.

The stack of "things to do" was so overwhelming that the landscape of my vision was blurred. I needed to "sit with my Savior" and have my heart and eyes readjusted for all this newness and period of transition.

If you have walked with the Savior for any length of time, you have probably come to a point where occasionally He seems distant and unconcerned with what you're experiencing in life. It may seem and feel that way, but He is as close to us as our heartbeat. But we need to choose to look for Him, regardless of our emotional status.

Being quiet can be difficult sometimes, can't it! But it's oh so necessary if we want our emotional equilibrium to be adjusted to "steady."

To be completely honest, I was lonely. I chose a comfortable chair in our family room. I remember that both chairs were blue and white stripped. It was at the far end of the room by a large window. This area of the room was cozy, and I had arranged the two chairs to face each other with a glass end table at an angle in between. It isn't critical that you see this arrangement, but it provided a lovely setting for two people to chat.

I settled my body into one of the chairs and discovered that I had neglected to make myself a cup of tea. Moments later the tea kettle was boiling and the thought dawned on me. I'm alone, I feel alone, but I'm not <u>really</u> alone ... Jesus is with me. The sweetest thought popped into my mind; I'll make two cups of tea. One for me and one for Jesus.

Yes, I located two nice china tea cups, made two cups of tea, and paraded them over to where I'd be sitting.

The presence of the "other cup of tea" was a VIVID reminder that I wasn't alone.

Time passed, and as I read God's Word and had a long chat about my new experience, my new location, and wondered what new plans would God have in store for my husband and I.

When I've shared this with others, they often ask ... was the cup of liquid tea still in the cup? Of course, it was! But the fact that the tea was still present didn't discourage the fact that Jesus was "very present" with me.

But the placement of the tea cup for Him brought the reality to me that morning that even though we can't see Him with our visible eyes, we can see Him with our inner spiritual eyes, and know in our heart He wouldn't leave us for a moment. And seeing the tea cup brought that reality alive for me that morning.

Just recently, I was sharing this event with a lovely young woman named Alysia. We were both enjoying a cup of tea on the back patio together sharing stories of our encounters with our Savior. This young woman just oozed with the Savior's joy and delight. Time passed, and off she went to be with some other friends for the evening. This was on a Friday afternoon.

On Sunday as I returned from church, I went out to the back patio to open the awning as it was a very warm, sunny day. Then ... there it was ... a new TEA CUP placed in the center of the patio table with this message on a wee note above the cup:

"Having tea with my sweet Dianne. Jesus"

My heart stopped and my eyes got enlarged. I couldn't believe my eyes. It was as though Jesus stopped by and left me a note to say He had been there to see me and enjoy tea.

Who in the world knew about my teacup episode that happened years earlier? It was this Alysia ... it *had* to be her. I phoned her immediately to confirm my suspicions of the precious delivery she had made when I was at church. She had to drive at least 20 minutes to get this cup to me.

What a beautiful reminder it is of the memory of having made an extra cup of tea for Him years ago.

This young woman's thoughtfulness resurrected the beautiful memory of the past. The next time you feel a bit lonely, make two cups of tea for your heart's pleasure.

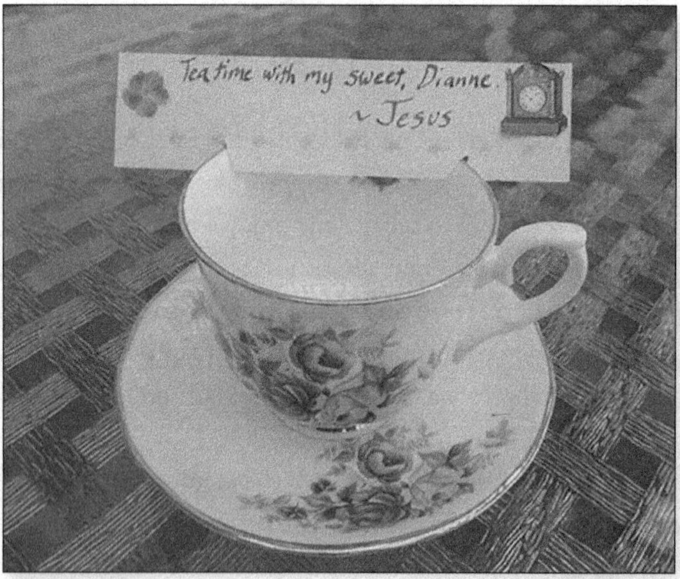

Tea time with my sweet, Dianne.
~ Jesus

Roses in the Bushes

Most everyone goes through a season of depression in their lives. Our latest move was to the northwest, and I was experiencing a type of grieving.

Every move involves more than just packing and transporting possessions to a new locale: You leave well-established friendships; You leave the "known" for the "unknown."

I was like a plant moved and deposited into fresh new soil. My emotions and countenance looked droopy, and I felt out of sorts for several months. In this new soil, I was well out of my comfort zone. Such was my condition!

On a particularly rainy, overcast day the sky was a collage of grey gloom. Turning on more lights in our home didn't help. So, I thought some fresh air might assist raising me to a higher emotional altitude.

What I missed was the people, and the many loving responsibilities in ministry I had with others ... and now I was alone. My husband was at work.

I headed out the door with a sweater and the necessary rain gear. The day reflected my mood, and I didn't even feel like talking.

But the Lord knows our "thoughts" just as clear as our spoken words. On this walk I reminisced about the many changes and adjustments my husband and I were again facing.

On my previous walks there was a cute little cul-de-sac that I would often venture into. The trees had begun adorning themselves with touches of crayon-like colors.

As I turned a corner into this secluded area, I noticed a large pile of freshly cut grass, and something caught my attention. As I approached the cut grass, I saw two bright red freshly cut, long-stemmed roses.

I couldn't believe it. I looked around wondering if someone has just laid these roses on the grass clippings and had forgotten to pick them up. I waited for a while, but no one appeared. These clippings were not in a well-traveled location. It was odd.

Then, as God would have it, He brought to mind all that I had been thinking about: the sadness; the people I missed; and more.

My heart just leapt for joy in the thought that, "these were roses from God for me" came to my mind. He knew just how to touch my heart and my life on that walk to remind me that He cared, and that He knew all about this transition.

I slowly picked up the two rose stems and hurried home.

One rose I kept in a vase. The other rose I pressed and placed it behind glass in a delicate gold frame.

The date was November 24th, 2005. This gift brought a "tender anticipation" of hope that good things were ahead, and to let God order the events of the coming years.

I'm grateful God gave me the presence of mind to "seal the rose under glass" as a cherished reminder of his tender and compassionate care through the stress and transitions in our lives.

Each time I look at this framed rose, my heart goes back to the time when God's love came near ... near enough to hold in my hand.

A Pharmacy Letter: A Prescription of Encouragement

Don't you just love it when on an ordinary day, in an ordinary way, God constructs an extraordinary adventure? Nothing is ordinary when God shows up with His surprise.

This day began in a dentist's chair, well, patient's chair. In pain and uncomfortable, I waited for her diagnosis. The dentist was tiny–in fact she could have placed both of her hands in my mouth for a look-around. She had skillfully demonstrated her skill in giving me "almost painless" Novocain three days earlier.

Before proceeding any further, let's agree that we know when the "needle" is on its way by the fact the dentist distracts us with a question, and cleverly hides the thin needle from our direct vision.

Well, I knew what was coming and I was ready for her. I closed my eyes – the coward that I am.

As she was about to administer the freezing gel, she pulled out the needle like a gunslinger's gun in the wild west, aimed and fired, and all was well.

I often use laughter in order to relax … for me and for those who are attending to me medically. In the sixty seconds it took for the Novocain to numb my jaw, one of my husband's comments about physicians and dentists came to my mind.

My husband says that he never minds going to a dentist, it's the doctors he is afraid of. I asked him why? His immediate and well-thought-of comment was, "A dentist has to stay in your mouth. A doctor can go anywhere on your body!"

This comment brought the dentist and her assistant (whom I refer to as Susie suction) into hysterical laughter.

After thirty minutes of being horizontal, I was more than ready to hit the lift off button.

Have you ever considered the reasons they position you in that troubling horizontal position?

My guess is that once you're down, they've got you right where they want you ... and unless you're a gymnast, you'll not escape their grasp. Yes, I know there are good reasons, and one of them isn't to help you sleep.

I arose and exited the clinic. Now equipped with a prescription for antibiotics, I was about to drive to our pharmacy not far from our home.

However, it was near dinner time, and I had prepared dinner before my appointment, so I thought I would go home and have quick bite to eat.

Chewing very carefully, I swallowed some of the meal and made a quick exit to our local pharmacy.

As always, the pharmacists were very personable and efficient. It took them five minutes to prepare my prescription.

Normally I just thank them and head out the door. However, this time it was different.

I was amazed how quickly my prescription had been filled, and I found myself giving some verbal encouragement to one of the pharmacy staff.

I also realized that this woman must also encounter some not-so-nice customers throughout the day. As I expressed my appreciation, my words were accepted as though they were pain killers for what she and the other staff members often experience.

She was overjoyed with my words of affirmation, and was quick to tell me that she would share my positive comments with her associates and supervisor.

As I exited the store, my immediate thought was that I should write a letter of encouragement one day and bring it in for the staff to have on hand for those not-so-good days ... and their dealing with the impatient clients.

When pulling into our garage I realized that I had forgotten to take both prescriptions, I had only picked up the one. The Novocain was wearing off, and the right side of my mouth was becoming uncomfortable.

I finished my dinner quickly so I could return to the pharmacy once again to get the remainder of my pills.

I noticed my computer was on, and I quickly typed four short paragraphs of gratitude—describing how the staff at this pharmacy was efficient, caring, personable, and so kind in the manner in which they filled my order.

The printer cooperated, and my words of praise were there in black and white.

I had less than fifteen minutes before the pharmacy closed. Now, it was my turn to hand over my "prescription of encouragement."

The gal at the counter was waiting for me! I told her I was sorry I had neglected to pick everything up. Her countenance welcomed me beyond belief. She shared how she had passed along my kind words to the staff and they were beaming with joy.

Now ... the good stuff! I handed her my letter and her eyes became like soccer balls. Our conversation stopped while she read my letter. Smiles were seen all over the pharmacy as others looked on with amazement. Then it was my turn to be surprised.

She handed me two little gifts, face cream and cleansing wipes. These gifts were from her to me for taking the time to share with her my thoughtful observations I had about their staff—not only for today, but on prior occasions as well.

We embraced and I smiled as I exited the store and made my way home.

We never know what others are experiencing. This dialogue took less than five minutes, and yet it brought strength and encouragement to the entire pharmacy staff.

The story doesn't end here. At the bottom of my letter, I included my phone number. I really have no idea why I did that as they have my number in their files, but I did it none-the-less.

The following day, I received this text from one of the pharmacists: "Good morning, Dianne, it's Alex from the pharmacy. What lovely feedback you gave us. You really uplifted the staff's morale. Really appreciate your kind words."

My pharmacy visit was for filling a prescription, so they could make "my day!" But it ended up with my letter making "their day."

I'm reminded again that God orders our steps daily. He desires that we see others through the lens of His love. We can do so by affirming and bringing refreshment to others in this busy world. Here is a passage from Proverbs 11:25–"The generous soul will be made rich, and he who waters will also be watered himself."

Yes, water refreshes our lips, but a good word refreshes our soul!

When God Says No

"The greatest crisis we ever face is the surrender of our will."

It is no secret we live in a very **self-centered** world. We don't have to go far to experience attitudes such as *me-first*, or *I deserve it*. Of course, as babies we are the center of attention, and simply think this should happen to us for the rest of our lives.

As we age, our childish cravings for attention become a full-blown addiction centered on **it's all about me** … if our nature hasn't been changed by God through a Divine rebirth. When God, through the Holy Spirit, comes into a life, our nature undergoes a radical transformation, like a caterpillar turns into a chrysalis and then into a beautiful butterfly.

Who knew that accepting Jesus Christ as my personal Savior many years ago would be the best, most powerful decision I've ever made. What started as a peace and inner joy I had never felt before, also came with an assurance of moving into His presence the moment my earthly life ends. From that moment onwards, I really began to live life to the fullest.

This experience is like a spiritual "adoption," and we are brought into not just a relationship with God, but into His family. Through this transaction, God places within us the start of a new DNA or divine nature – complete with new thoughts, attitudes, and better desires.

We should not be surprised when we learn that our lives are starting to look different to others. The process is not automatic, since we have to continually yield or give up parts of ourselves, and participate in God's renewing of our minds, hearts and behavior. Through the growth process – acknowledged by regular reading of the Bible – we are able to understand more truths and apply them to our lives. Thus, things we once enjoyed and found important, no longer hold the same meaning.

What were once the *desires of our heart* can be transformed as well. I should point out that I've found yielding my will to God has sometimes been an agonizing process. God loves us beyond our comprehension, and His mercy and tenderness are incredible; but the following Scripture passages tells us that "His ways are not like ours."

- Isaiah 55:8 *"For My thoughts are not your thoughts, neither are your ways My ways," declares the Lord."*
- Proverbs 19:21 *"There are many plans in a man's heart, nevertheless the Lord's counsel—that will stand."*
- Proverbs 16:9 *"A man's heart plans his way, but the Lord directs his steps."*
- Proverbs 20:24 *"A man's steps are of the Lord; how then can a man understand his own way?"*

These verses have not only changed my life, but have continued to give me a perspective on how God works. In my case, to shape my attitude with desires that will bring glory and honor to Him.

He is so worthy of our love and trust because He always has our best in mind. I say that gently, because what is good for us (like medicine when we're ill) doesn't always feel good at the time as we apply it, but it brings wonderful results.

My journey with God grew over the years through reading and applying His Word into my life. I gradually came to realize and accept how much He cared about every detail of my life. His love extended to my daily activities and decisions as they played out in life's various circumstances.

After about five years in my walk with God, a deep yearning for children began to formulate in my heart. The hunger for starting a family of our own was getting hard to ignore. At the core of this yearning was the fact that I had been adopted and longed for the stability of children to call my own.

We had been married a few years, and at this point in our married life, I began to struggle. We prayed and waited. The waiting continued for about seven years. The struggle was emotional and began to grow. Of course, our desire was perfectly normal and honorable. However, God had other plans.

I remember a discussion my husband and I had about perhaps adopting a baby or a young child. He wasn't on board with this suggestion. It wasn't that he opposed the idea, but he just felt no peace about it.

In my frustration I exercised my human intervention. In other words, I attempted to *help* God, like Abraham's wife Sarah, and manipulate another way of having a child. I'm ashamed to admit this, but this story requires complete openness in the "honesty department."

I obtained an "adoption application" from the internet, and did so without my husband's knowledge.

Yes, we can often try to "get what we want" through other means. This is called ***manipulation***," plain and simple, but like all our decisions if carried out, begin a series of consequences that affect us for a long time.

I hid the application in my desk drawer in our bedroom. One morning, I pulled out the application to begin completing the questionnaire. Deep within, I felt as though I was "sneaking around my husband's wishes." To make matters worse, I sensed I was trying to go behind God's back (how ridiculous is that) and get what I wanted ... one way or another.

God is merciful and kind ... if we allow Him to be. My "conviction and uneasiness" were real, and came from deep within my heart. I knew I was trying to orchestrate this *baby* in my own way. This was exactly the same tactic Sarah used to obtain a child. We can be so critical of her attempt to bring things to pass in her way and her time, rather than wait on God to do what He wants and has planned for our lives.

> Isaiah 64:4 *"Since ancient times no one has heard, no ear has perceived, no eye has seen any God besides you,* **Who acts on behalf of those who wait for Him."**

WOW ... God acts on our behalf, if we wait for Him.

May I invite you to stop reading this story and ponder the above statement regarding your own desires? When I stop and take time to meditate on this truth, my mind and heart are refreshed, and I am pulled closer to God with this thought:

God has the plans, purpose, and the timing of events in our lives.

Reflecting on some of my decisions, I realize how often I took matters into my own hands – rather than choosing to wait and trust Him. It's never easy to wait on God, but it's *safer to wait and trust* than to experience and live with the consequences of our hasty, not-so-wise choices.

Yes, God is merciful, and he often allows lingering consequences to remind us to "get with His program" and not try and exercise our own will, over His.

Now I should add some critical circumstances where God began to show me what He was "up to" in our lives and "family plans."

In a quiet way one morning when I was reading His Word, I thought of the following:

> *"I know you love children, but had you thought that everyone that comes to your front door is a child, sent by Me (God), for you to love?"*

Weeks later a couple came to stay in our home for a few days. I had some discussion with the woman about my desire. As these friends were exiting our home at the front door, she turned to me and said:

> *"I know you love children, but had you thought that everyone that comes to your front door is a child for you to love?"*

Here is another spot for you to stop reading ... and let those two comments marinate in your mind. My friend had quoted what God had spoken to my heart weeks earlier. Talk about a "confirmation" from God, this was in bold print.

There is one more event that needs to be included in this period of waiting. I had thought that perhaps there was something wrong with me physically that needed a physician's attention. So, I made an appointment with a doctor.

Oddly enough, my best friend's mother-in-law was a nurse and worked for this doctor. A few days prior to my appointment, she phoned me and asked me to come for lunch. My only contact with this lovely woman was at church and we had only said our hellos on Sunday. We really didn't know each other, but what a kind invitation.

I accepted her lunch offer and showed up bright as a button at her front door. She was gracious and so welcoming. We had a delightful lunch and rather than a dessert, she presented me with a very penetrating question that just about took my breath away.

The conversation drifted toward my upcoming appointment with the physician. She was concerned for me and wanted to know the nature of my appointment. I thought that odd, especially over lunch, and since she would have asked the same question when I arrived at the waiting room days later.

She had such a warm and understanding way about her, and I felt safe to share my concerns. What I never expected was her response. We often wish God would speak to us verbally. Well, this lunch hour was His chosen spot, and with the chosen person who would be very "direct and tender" with me. She asked why I wanted to see a doctor. I shared my concerns about the possibility that my body wasn't able to house a baby and wondered if the physician could help me in some way.

This was her response:

"Dianne, is the Lord the lord of your life? Is He really in charge?"

My response was "Yes, as best I know, He is in charge of my life."

She asked one other question I shall never forget. "Dianne, is He Lord of your womb?"

My mind, heart and will were "silenced." There was no need to say anything more. God poignantly showed me that He Himself was in charge of all of me. He could open or close my womb at His discretion and design.

Another miracle took place in my heart. It was a "heart surgery" that no one could accomplish but my Creator-God. He assured me that even though His answer was *no*, it came with a positive slant. This spiritual heart surgery enabled me to change my perspective, and God showed me that I had been limiting my request.

You see, I wanted a child that weighed about six pounds, eight ounces. God began introducing me to hundreds of children, for me to love and pour into their lives. As I chose to view everyone He brings to the front door of my life and in my circumstance as "someone God has sent for me to love," I realized that **everyone is a child**. We are all just different heights, sizes and ages. Everyone needs to be loved … because everyone is made in His image.

I was reminded of this when reading a sign at an optometrist's office when I began wearing glasses. It's priceless.

Dear God: I can see you much better with my new glasses!

It wasn't my womb that needed correction, it was my "eyes." God needed to alter my vision to see things from His perspective. Over the years He **has given us children**, many children. Although they are not from my body, they are loved from my heart.

Such is the extent of God's power to change. The Bible tells us that the Savior of the world was divinely placed within the Virgin Mary's womb, an embryo of God, who became a human being. He came to show us Who God the Father is, and to show us how much God loves each of us.

My prayer is that this "journey of waiting" will encourage you to turn to, and trust the all-knowing, all-powerful Creator God Who loves you more than you could possibly know.

It's now been many years ago that all this transpired, and if you would ask me "Would you still prefer God's will, or your own?" My resounding response would be HIS WILL!

An Adoption Story – Part 1

Have you ever wondered, *"Was my life planned?"* or *"Was I a surprise to my parents?"* or *"Could I have been plan B instead of plan A?"* Such thoughts are usually not shared on your birthday while opening gifts.

My story begins as an unwanted baby who entered this world with the absence of parents. I was an unplanned creation in the womb of a single woman, but I know that my appearance was right on schedule. Though given away at birth, I prefer to use the term surrendered upon delivery.

My birth-mother had already raised a family, and her 'one evening affair' had blossomed into more than she could practically and financially accommodate. By the world's standards, I was the penalty for a mistake.

But this is only the beginning of my story. For many parents their babies are surprise packages – to which you could say, "Amen, you got that right!" You may never really know how *"planned"* you were, or if you were planned at all. But let me tell you. You were not a mistake!

My original parents made a bad emotional decision one night, one they both would live to regret. But it was part of God's plan to use their *"mistake,"* and weave a tiny baby into the fabric of His wonderful purpose. God takes great delight in the birth and life of every child.

In my first two years, I traveled a lot ... though not for pleasant holiday excursions. Rather, I was an infant gypsy – in and out of foster homes. No one wanted to adopt a baby with a medical condition like mine.

A particular social worker in Ohio was aware of me, and she felt prompted to introduce me to a client seeking to adopt a baby. My mother remembers the words well, "I have just the child for you!"

Though only two years old, I was instinctively aware and appreciative of any positive introductory comments made on my behalf.

The day arrived, and I was introduced to my "new mom." My life-long belongings were contained in the little brown bag much like a sack lunch.

My new mom knew nothing about my infectious draw toward people, or my fledgling social personality, but it was soon discovered on the way to my new home. She remembers how I waved with delight at all the truck drivers we passed in the car.

At a young age I was introduced to Sunday school and began learning "about" Jesus. My mom remembers me looking up at about four years of age, and having a conversation in the backyard with my head tilted upward toward the sky and saying, "I know You're up there, but I just can't see You."

Even at four, God was working in my heart to produce a yearning to know the One who created me and loved me ... even when no one else had.

I was kept as a "secret" from my entire birth family ... except for a half-brother who was nineteen years older than I. He actually gave me a name at my birth before they escorted me away from the delivery room.

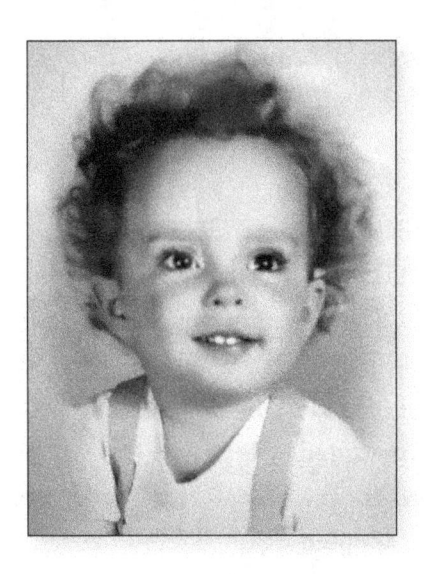

Fast forward nineteen years to age 21. I went to the city's "Family and Children's Adoption Services" to inquire about my birth-mother. I loved my adoptive parents, but my natural curiosity about my background, and information as to any possible health issues prompted my interest.

I learned that due to the state laws in Ohio, that all of the information about my past had been sealed.

My adopted mother had coached me beforehand as to the questions the agency may ask me in my attempt to locate information about the birth mother. For example: "Why was I adopted" in the first place.

Perhaps the mother couldn't afford to keep me. Maybe she didn't want any more children. Or, perhaps I was illegitimate. What I knew for sure was, I wasn't on my birth parents' hearts.

This first appointment did answer: "Yes, I was not a planned child, and I was referred to as *illegitimate*." With tears overflowing, I exited the agency and just stood on the sidewalk trying to digest the truth about the purpose of my arrival into this world.

Illegitimate! Unplanned! Unwanted! In those fleeting moments I felt lost, unloved and disconnected by those words and their meaning.

These emotions faded in the truth of the commitment and love my adopted mom had given me all these years. You see, she was my "real mom" ... who took me and my brown bag of belongings into her home. I grew in the womb of one woman, but was nurtured in the heart of another.

My new mom was the one "designed and selected by God" for this seemingly unwanted little girl.

Fast forward another twenty years, and laws that had previously prevented adopted children from seeing or accessing their records had now been changed.

My mother shared this news about the change of laws, and together with prayer, we began the search for a name, a birth place, and a mother who had surrendered her daughter.

The investigating court documents yielded my birth name. We found six people with my given "last name" at birth, and a letter was sent to these six individuals.

The purpose and content of the letter was to thank them for giving me up at birth, and for granting me an opportunity to experience the love of a family.

Within days, one of the recipients phoned to acknowledge that he may be my step-brother ... the one 19 years older, and who had actually given me my name. He was the only one who had held me before I was given away to the adoption agency.

He was the one and the only one from my birth family who had attempted any investigation or search as to my whereabouts! I had no idea that he had been trying to undo the court's stipulation of secrecy for years.

After all, both he and I shared the same birth-mother, and he had never stopped wondering where his little sister was, and how her life had unfolded?

Forty years had passed by, and now, through this letter and a telephone call, a new relationship would begin to emerge.

My step-brother made contact with our birth mother letting her know about this discovery. Talk about "surprises," this one took the cake! After I was born, she had asked her son to keep this "little baby" a secret for the rest of his life, and he had honored her request.

But now, after receiving my "thank you" letter, the secret would begin to unravel and be revealed.

Many women can bear children, but that doesn't mean they're destined to be mothers. I loved my adoptive mom and was devoted to her.

I wouldn't allow anything to jeopardize this relationship ... even if it pertained to information about my past.

It was almost Thanksgiving–how appropriate. I returned to Ohio to visit my parents, and we "just happened" to be watching a television program on adoption ... and I just knew this was the moment to share with them what had happened.

As my parents listened to the news, to everyone's surprise and amazement, we discovered that the man – my half-brother – lived just two miles from my adoptive parents.

An even greater surprise was that they knew him quite well, since he had serviced and repaired their lawn mowers for years. SURPRISES are all over this story.

Within days I contacted my birth mother to make arrangements to meet her.

I pause here for a moment. How would YOU feel if you were in HER shoes? She had given birth to me 40 years earlier, but chosen (wisely, I feel) not to see, or hold me. Now, this once little one making herself known, and the air is thicker than a brick.

If you were the adoptive mother, what would you be thinking? Amazingly, my mom was pleased to come along with me. She actually wanted to meet the woman who gave away her infant baby girl, not in desperation, but in love.

I surely didn't want to face this delicate moment and reunion alone. I had no idea what to expect.

Somehow my adoptive mother knew, and could comprehend my kaleidoscope of emotions. Without any prompting at all, she offered to accompany me for a visit to meet my unknown family.

The revelation of a 40 year-long secret was just two miles away, and the revelation of my identity would soon be exposed.

As we approached the home of my step-brother, my pulse quickened. My heart was racing as if in the Indy 500! How was this moment even possible after forty years? There has never been a truer instance of the verse from Luke 1:37, *"For with God, nothing shall be impossible."*

The first few moments of our meeting were subdued. We could have heard a pin drop when all of our eyes met, and it seemed that no one was breathing a breath, or saying a word. Is this what happens when reality and profound disbelief encounter each other?

In fact, it was a divine appointment ... arranged forty years prior, by an all-knowing, and all-caring and loving God.

We gradually and intermittently took turns exchanging comments and questions and staring at each other following each answer. It must have seemed quite humorous, because it was apparent that no one wanted to be caught in the act of "continual eye surveillance."

These were tender moments that would be etched and forever recorded in my heart. I remembered that in the previous months I wasn't sure I was ready to meet "this woman."

An Adoption Story – Part 2

Prior to meeting with my step-brother and birth-mother, my husband addressed my fear of the forthcoming meeting by encouraging me with the explanation that I was the only one on this earth that could reassure this birth-mother of God's forgiveness, and express my gratefulness to her that she had the heart to release me into God's care.

Now, sitting in a home, which only a few weeks prior, had seemed like an infinite distance away, we needed to bring what seemed like hours of visiting to a close … for now.

As we were getting ready to leave, a memory was created – one that will be forever engraved on my heart. I saw both of my "mothers" exchanging their parting words – in essence talking behind my back!

"Thank you for having this little baby so I could have a daughter," my mom said, and included me as third in a group hug – as a grown up "secret baby," a gift beyond measure, and causing my heart to fill to overflowing.

Here's a funny …. I recall back to my grade school years. I recollect a classmate's comment about my being "adopted". "You don't **look adopted**" she said. To which I replied, "Well, you don't **look natural.**" I was quick to inform this gal that I knew I was wanted … because I was **chosen**. After all, parents of natural-born children only get pot–luck!

To my thinking, and perhaps yours, my life wasn't a "gift" to my birth parents. My arrival was neither planned nor expected.

However, I was "on time" from God's perspective. Yes, they made a mistake, but God didn't. God created me ... and you for a purpose. While we may know some facts about Him, He knows each one of us intimately. Sadly, not all who were designed by Him know Him in a "relational way."

Even though I was now all grown up, there still remained a "child-like void" in my life. To an outsider, I likely appeared a happy person. In reality I was very insecure, lonely and without a real purpose. There was a "presence" missing within me ... a gaping hole that couldn't be filled.

Though baptized as an infant, I attended confirmation classes, and was accustomed to being in church. In my late teen years I pulled away from church as religion seemed irrelevant, and God seemed so impersonal and uninterested in my existence.

A dear friend shared two great truths about life. First, she was the first who told me the truth about Santa Claus ... we won't go any further ... just in case some of you still put cookies out on December 24th.

Second, that God sent His Son Jesus, wrapped in human flesh, to die on a cross ... to take the punishment for my sin. Wow! Talk about a good-news / bad-news announcement.

I never liked the word sin ... still don't. But it was true. There was no denying that I was a "sinner." Deep down I knew there was a separation between me and a perfect and holy God. I would often try to appease myself by thinking *'I'm not as bad as other people'*.

But deep within, I knew I wasn't good enough to enter heaven. Who is? I told my friend that I believed in God ... wasn't that good enough? James 2 verse 19 took care of that answer: "Even Satan and his demons believe, but I know their destination."

My friend told me that Jesus took the penalty for my sins when He died on the Cross, and that I could be forgiven for anything and everything from my past, present and future – if I allowed Him to.

She helped me understand that my entire life was visible on God's computer screen, and His computer had been recording everything I had ever said, thought or did.

By accepting the fact that Jesus took my place on the cross, and fully understanding that I could never erase my sin on my own – I'd be forgiven. It's as though God hits the DELETE BUTTON and completely erases every record of my <u>every wrong</u>.

It took time for my mind and heart to absorb all this. Deep within I had fears and a troubled spirit that I couldn't just brush away. It was my lingering fear of death and dying that frightened me. I never wanted to know the truth about what would happen to me when I died.

After all, our souls (the real us) were created to live forever ... somewhere! How easily we want to ignore the "big elephant" in the room ... and want to sweep it under the rug.

The fact is that one day every one of our hearts will cease to beat ... and we will leave this earth. Millions of gravestones around the world bear testimony that people die everywhere ... and at all ages.

That realization allowed me to discover that God was, in fact, very much interested and does wish to direct my steps. From that point forward my life took on new purpose and meaning.

God brings people together and orchestrates circumstances in everyone's life, and He desires a response from them... toward Him.

Not long after our conversation, I saw someone on TV talking about the same thing my friend shared with me, and I knew God was trying to get my attention.

I hadn't really looked up to talk with God since I was four, but I made the decision right then and knelt down to talk with Him and asked Jesus for His forgiveness. I asked God to come into my life, to make me new and help me to follow Him.

His offer of forgiveness is like the "great exchange" I call it ... giving our sins over to Christ, accepting that He died for all of them (past, present & future) so that I could go free from judgment and be free to finally get to know God and have a relationship with Him.

This salvation, or being born again, was His gift to me ... as it is to anyone who turns from their way of living to His way. For years I sat in church trying to **'be good'** ... thinking I was 'in' as far as heaven was concerned.

But once I realized the difference between *doing* ... rather than simply *accepting* what had already been DONE ... for me, a great peace took over. It makes sense that God, our Creator, knows what's really best for us, because He loves us unconditionally.

He took me, just like my adopted mother and dad had, JUST AS I WAS. There was no cleaning myself up for Him. It will take a lifetime of 'tidying up to look more like His Son' while still here on earth.

When I breathe my last, I'll just move into His presence. For Christians dying, it just means we've moved to a new and better location.

Well, you've been privy to my first birth (a human, natural birth) ... then my human adoption by my parents. And now, my second birth (where God gave me new life ... a life that now could respond to Him).

Regardless of the circumstances surrounding your birth, God designed "you" in someone's womb. He fashioned you individually and intricately ... with your own personality, your own appearance, and your unique body structure. YOU are a "masterpiece" of His design!

I may have been "unplanned" and "unwanted" by two people, but God had plans for me in spite of the circumstance of my birth. It was now possible for me to stop wondering about who I was, why I was born, and what was my purpose in life.

I was "not a mistake" as I thought, but delightfully fashioned by my Creator with purpose beyond my imagination. <u>And He has designed each of you ... with that same delight</u>.

The disconsolate young woman standing, crying in front of an adoption agency after learning that she was "illegitimate" was now shedding tears of joy.

Through my friend, I was now learning and absorbing Biblical truths that brought changes to my everyday living. This was just the start of a journey planned even before my conception.

My mother developed many medical issues in her latter life requiring full-time care from her adopted daughter. This gift of having my mother in my home to care for brought me joy, fulfillment, and the privilege of a lifetime.

Here is where the fabric of "Divine providence," orchestrated with all its beauty, began weaving a new twist of events.

I felt honored that this would be my opportunity to extend love and care for the woman who gave so much to adopt me. She wasn't a young woman when she chose to do that.

At the age of 97½, just three months before she died, the adopted little girl, now a woman, had the privilege of praying with her mother and assist her in receiving Christ as her personal Savior, accepting His forgiveness, and adoption into God's family. The "gift of adoption" had now travelled through the full range of life's journey.

It seemed as though the adoption experience that began with a "chosen mother" for two daughters (myself and an *adorable* adopted sister), now came full-circle. The first daughter had the privilege of being chosen by God to assist in His adoption "of her mother" into His family.

My mother was herself adopted into God's family! She too was born in the heart of God before creation (Psalm 139). God had ordained all these "adoptions" for many Divine purposes.

My story is of a gal who had thought her life was nothing but a tragic mistake due to someone else's recklessness. However, the real blunder was not understanding a wonderful truth: that each of us has been created by God's purpose and design. Psalm 139

LOOKING THROUGH THE LENS OF . . .

The greatest act of love was expressed at the Cross ... offering everyone a clean slate ... with nothing left to condemn us, so that when each of us stands before Him one day (**and everyone will!**), we can point to Jesus stating that He alone took the punishment for our sins. Nothing will be held against us.

Jesus Offers Himself Freely ... as a **Gift** to You

Gifts are wonderful, aren't they? Whether at Christmas, birthdays, or "just because" gifts from a friend who loves us. Gifts are meant to be <u>received</u> ... they are not gifts if they are <u>earned</u>.

Why not take Him up on His "gift-offer" and enjoy the greatest decision you'll ever make! In Acts 13:38, 39 we read: "In this man Jesus there is forgiveness for your sins. Everyone who believes in Him is freed from all guilt and declared right with God."

The following passage in John 14:6, also adds, "I am the way and the truth and the life. No one comes to the Father except through Me."

Flying First Class

I am neither a frequent flyer on the airlines, nor do I possess a frequent flyer card like my husband. My flying is usually limited to "cattle car" ... at least that's what it feels like when carefully positioned in economy class for more than 4 hours.

In my limited flying experience, it seems everyone wants to load their larger carry-on bags into the overhead bins which usually disrupts the flow, and delays the boarding of passengers. For this reason, I try and travel light.

On one occasion I was boarding a plane to return to California from Columbus, Ohio. One has to admit there is a distinct similarity between herding animals on a farm, and loading people on an airplane. The airline personnel try to make the process smooth, moving several hundred people in an orderly fashion through a deliberately narrow portal, and do so with as much grace and speed as possible. Let's just say that not everyone wishes to cooperate or follow their guidelines.

Once inside the aircraft, a well-groomed flight attendant directed me toward my assigned seat. Since there were a couple of hundred people behind me, I slipped into my seat and belted myself in quickly.

I just started to relax a little when another passenger approached my aisle and gave me "the look." You know, the "you're in my seat look." The passenger held out their boarding pass, and wouldn't you know it ... their seat number was the same as mine. By this time the cabin crew noticed the kink in the flow of traffic in the aisle and approached us both. If I were a child, my first words would have been, "I was here first," but I held my tongue ... which ... at this point was a good thing to get hold of.

The other passenger was a bit more forceful in their tone of voice. The flight attendant looked at me in despair and asked me to follow her, which I did.

My new assigned seat was now closer to the front of the plane. Again, I sat down and secured my seat belt in position ready for our in-flight safety movie. I had no more than drawn a sigh of relief, when another fellow passenger approached me with the same "look."

I had just memorized my new assigned seat number which I shared with them and, you guessed it, they had the identical number. This same crew member noticed the situation occurring again, and now she was as frustrated as I was.

Round two of "the seat-relocation process" began, and I waited for her next directive, thinking she would leave me seated and relocate the *other* individual since I had already been inconvenienced in a prior move.

However, her reaction was different this time. She paused, looked at me intently and said "follow me." Somewhat like a salmon, it seemed we were travelling upstream in the aisle heading in the opposite direction. When we got to a space where the two of us could look each other in the eyes, she thanked me profusely for being so accommodating and understanding. I was a bit inwardly embarrassed because I didn't *feel* so understanding.

Shouldn't we be glad people can't read our minds? I know God knows our thoughts and He was working in the "patience" part of character-building in me that morning.

Then we arrived at my final seating assignment–FIRST CLASS! Not just first class, I was seated in the first row of the first-class cabin.

I turned to ask her the "why question," but before I could speak, she told me that because I was so patient and never complained verbally, she wanted to reward me with a first-class seat.

Oh my, was I ever a happy camper! Even as I was fastening my seat belt, I paused to wonder if I could be in another's preassigned seat. At last, I thought, I was "home in the right seat." I am sure my face was the picture of gratefulness!

I remember that my seat was on the aisle and the seat beside me was empty. There was so much space in this section that I could have laid down and had a stack of books next to me.

The inflight safety instructions were announced at this time and I listened to every word, especially due to the fact I was sitting in first class, and I wondered if they had different arrangements for exiting an aircraft.

Then a pilot appeared in front of me and proceeded to sit in the vacant seat next to me! My goodness, this man was dressed in the airline uniform, hat and all; and I wondered why he was sitting in the first row–next to me? Wasn't he supposed to be in the cockpit?

I soon discovered when speaking to him why he was sitting next to me. He had piloted the plane on the incoming flight and was now headed home. Obviously, he was allowed to sit in first class.

Engines started and we were soon up, up, and away. This nice-looking gentleman took off his hat and introduced himself to me. It did not take long for my ignorance of first-class travel to reveal itself, and I shared with him that I had never flown first class before. I must have sounded like an awestruck kid in a candy store.

This flight occurred when domestic airline travel still offered meals. I was first to receive a very nice meal served on fine china and silverware. It was incredible service with linens all over the place. I felt like a first-class queen. The only thing missing was a red rose.

After dinner, the off-duty pilot asked if I wanted another cup of tea. *Are you kidding, of course,* though I didn't say it like that, and responded with a refined "that would be lovely, thank you."

I could hardly believe all the benefits of first-class travel including the meal, the service, and now the tea. I was smiling from ear to ear, and almost could not take in everything that was happening. I managed to keep my emotions under control as well as my lips.

The flight would be about three and a half hours. After dinner I settled back for a relaxing flight. My pilot-seatmate made some general comments which I expected would be about general pleasantries. But I could tell by the direction and tone of the conversation, that he was not only physically tired, but he was tired of what life seemed to be offering him. It was obvious he was feeling depressed, and believe me, if a pilot is not well mentally, you want him seated outside the cockpit!

The conversation soon turned to spiritual matters. It did not take long for the conversation to turn to spiritual things. I introduced him to some thoughts about God. The flight seemed to go so fast, that the next thing I realized was that we were approaching our airport destination. For those hours, God opened up a dialogue about Him and how He cares for us. We spoke together for all those hours, and at the end of the flight the darkness had lifted, and the pilot felt incredibly full of joy.

He expressed how grateful that he and I had been seated together. I realized afresh that God had orchestrated several moves in order to get me to that first-class seat so that He could encourage this pilot through my words. I will never forget the experience.

But there is more. Just before landing, I shared with the pilot that I had always wanted to see what it was like to be in the cockpit. People are not allowed in that area, for good reasons. He listened and chuckled. The pilot left his seat next to me immediately upon the tires hitting the runway.

The flight landed safely and over the loud speaker I heard an announcement I've never heard before. They announced my name and asked me to remain seated after the landing. Oh my, what in the world had I done? People were leaving the aircraft and I was left alone in first class, wondering what in the world was going on.

Soon the off-duty pilot appeared and asked me to join him. He took me upstairs and escorted me to the cockpit of this Boeing 747. There were three people in the cockpit as the pilot and I entered. He introduced me and my "childhood wishes" were about to commence. I was breathless at the sight of all those knobs and buttons.

My first comments were that I had always prayed for the pilots before a flight, but after seeing the large array of buttons and dials on the instrument panel throughout the cockpit, I told them I would *really* be praying intently for every pilot on future flights.

They were very friendly and accommodating in their brief demo of procedures in the cockpit. Just when I thought the experience was about to end, the actual pilot of the flight got up out of his seat and offered the seat to me. I don't remember breathing as I took my place in the captain's chair. They wanted to take a photo, but guess what: the battery in my camera was flat.

Everyone laughed, but even though I don't have the photo, the scene is forever etched in my mind.

When we belong to God's family, He does indeed direct our steps (Psalm 37:23–NLT): "The LORD directs the steps of the godly. He delights in every detail of their lives."

Many times, His direction would seem like a detour, but He knows where He wants to place us for His good purposes.

Now, in case you are a frequent flyer ... and tend to fly first class ... and you need to be accompanied by an encourager who loves the Lord, please don't hesitate to make a reservation in my name. I'd be most delighted to sit next to you and share the goodness and care of the Lord.

May I Wash Your Feet?

This story has been germinating for many years, and it always brings tears to my eyes because of its special nature.

No one is the perfect parent, except God, the Father. His first two children, Adam and Eve—who lived in a perfect environment, had a perfect parent: God Himself. They, however, blew it big time. So, parents reading this, be encouraged.

My dad wasn't well versed on "affirmation." Since he was orphaned at eight when his mother died, he didn't have many mentors in his family. Most parents, regardless of what they have experienced, usually try to bring up their children the best they know how.

My story begins with this preface, and will, in the end, honor my dad.

My dad had an outgoing personality and was a very friendly. He could parade through a grocery store (which he did about four times a week) entertaining and befriending every clerk.

One time, as we were approaching the check out, I heard him refer to the cashier as Priscilla. Then as I approached, he would introduce me as his daughter, his first Priscilla. I had no idea I had so many namesakes.

Thanks to my husband's accrued air miles, I was able to visit my parents about four times a year. In addition to enjoying my time with them, it was an opportunity to tackle small and large cleanup projects around the home which allowed them to remain in their home.

After breakfast one morning, I took a cup of tea to my former bedroom (when I lived at home) and read my Bible. May I insert that I had been praying for my parents to receive Jesus Christ as their personal Savior for about 15 years.

My dad had absolutely no interest in God! That included any radio or television programs that brought God into focus. It took a number of years for God's wisdom to sink into my head and behavior to realize that my walk needed to match my talk!

In fact, there was little "talk" about Jesus as dad would either leave the conversation, or walk out of the room.

My father was diabetic and required insulin each day. By now my mother expertly handled this function twice every day for him. She was a very steady, strong-willed woman, and good at meeting my dad's needs.

I had no more than closed my Bible this particular morning when my mother gave a little knock on my door, and gently peeked in the door with a statement I shall never forget. I won't sermonize this, but there is one verse that will begin to come alive in the following paragraphs: "If I then, your Lord and Master, have washed your feet; you also ought to wash one another's feet."

My mom's words were: "There is something your dad would like you to do for him, and I can't do it." What???? My mom seemed to handle anything. Her morning injections were as smooth as ice. What was it that she couldn't do, that dad required?

I say that gingerly, because I was raised with many doubts that I could ever do anything right. Even if I mowed the lawn, he would be quick to point out a blade of grass that I had missed. My goodness, this had to be a BIG request.

"What is it?" I inquired. "He wants you to do his feet?" What that translates to is to clean and file down the almost ½ inch of fungus on his toenails. He was unable to do it himself.

He had seen a podiatrist (whom I love to refer to as a toenail doctor), and his procedure was very painful for my dad and he wasn't about to make a return appointment.

With the background I described earlier, can you sense the stress I was beginning to feel? Shortly thereafter, I approached my dad and asked him what he wanted in more detail.

I hadn't seen my dad's feet in years. You might think that odd, but if you think about it, we usually see people fully dressed: complete with shoes and socks.

He invited me to the living room and pulled off his socks to show me his feet, specifically, his toenails. I tried my best not to look shocked. The nails were at different heights and all filled with fungus that needed to be shaved down so they were smooth.

You might wonder how much experience I'd had in performing this podiatry skill. NONE! As I looked at his feet, my first thoughts were, I cannot do this. I don't know how.

Then it happened, God brought to my memory some of the verses I had just read in John 13. Words we may read in our devotional time aren't just words to *"leave on the page,"* they are to be *"worked out in the sneakers of living."*

God was preparing me for this new assignment.

All our God-assignments involve serving others–to bring honor and glory to God. In other words, our actions are to "make God look good."

The instant the reality of this verse hit home; I knew God was asking me to "attend to my dad's feet." This would involve not only cleaning his feet, but attending to and reducing the fungus under the nails.

Thus, my first idea that I shared with dad was that he needed to soak his feet in nice warm sudsy water. He was quite prepared as he had proper files, clippers and the works. I had prayed for over ten years for God to open up an opportunity to share Christ with him.

I had shared my story of becoming a Christian years prior, but with no positive response.

This evening was my "Divine Appointment and Divine Assignment." It was my time to "be the Gospel ... be Jesus to him."

My "Yes, I'll try," was my dad's good news for the day. I suggested that after supper I would get a container of nice clean warm water in which to soak his feet, and then attend to his tootsies! My dad's face lit up like a Christmas tree. He was more than on board for all of this.

After this brief introduction to his "tootsies" I went to my room to collect myself. I thought to myself, "How in the world can I do this? How can I get past the insecurity of the assignment? I wondered if this included feet?

God's Spirit instantly reminded me of two truths found in Philippians 2:13 and Philippians 4:13:

- "For it is God who works in you both to will and to do of His good pleasure. (Philippians 2:13)
- "I can do all things through Christ who strengthens me." (Philippians 4:13)

Dinner was over and the "foot event" was about to commence. But, how was I to do this? To me, this was an impossible task? The immediate answer was this: Dianne, pretend that your dad's feet were Jesus' feet.

That was a tall order, as well as it was my marching orders.

I'm glad mom shared his request in the afternoon, as it gave God and I time to interact about all of this and get the equipment ready. You'd have thought we were having a party … as my dad was "so enthusiastic."

Dad was anxious to get started and had himself all propped up on the sofa in the living room. Mom wanted to get in on all this too. They both seemed so relieved and excited about the potential activity. So, with my personality, I thought we might as well turn this into a "foot party."

Prepared with warm water, soap, wash cloth, nice towels, the soaking activity began. I soaped up his feet and gently rubbed them. That must have felt good as dad was all smiles about this time. Then I laid a towel on my lap and began patting dry his feet.

When I took the various files in my hand to begin, a wonderful thing happened in my heart that translated in my eyes. I began to see my dad's feet as though they were the feet of Jesus.

With gentle, yet firm strokes, I began the procedure of filing down each toenail. To my utter amazement they began to quickly reduce in size, and an hour later, all of his toenails were smooth to the touch and at a normal height and length. Afterwards I massaged his feet with a nice cream and covered his feet with clean white socks.

He was delighted!!! I was "over the moon" with relief. The best part of all this was that I never hurt him. God is so good.

This was the first of four cleaning sessions a year lasting for a little over twenty-five years. This was the first time in my life that my dad seemed appreciative of my efforts. Every time I came for a visit, we had a "foot party."

This foot party turned into a manicure of his hands. The party escalated so that even my mom wanted her feet and hands done too. Each party lasted about two hours – an hour for each of my "parent customers."

This isn't the end of the story. After praying thirty-eight years for my dad, and through twenty-five of those years, attending to his feet, my dad finally came to give his life to Christ just eleven days before the Lord took him home to heaven to be with his new-found Savior.

God touches others through our lives. He does use our lips, but often God works through loving others by "serving them" in whatever opportunity God opens up.

Many times, we're given the privilege of telling another about Jesus, and that's a wonderful joy. However, we also need to "show them Jesus" through loving service to them in whatever arena God brings to us. To demonstrate God's love requires our willingness to be changed ... and that is where the first miracle is initiated.

I think people would rather *experience* the love of God first-hand ... so that their hearts become most open to hearing about it!

Ordinary

I wonder if the title of this story has really gripped you? In today's marketing-driven world, people look for people and circumstances that are a "cut above" the ordinary. I seldom come across people who are "content and satisfied" with who and how God created them to be. Yes, it's a fallen world in which we live, that's blatantly obvious.

Generally speaking, we humans seem to long for the need to be successful, significant, important, irreplaceable, outstanding, remarkable, prosperous, at the top of our game, bestselling and notable.

For many, it's a life goal! We often strive, manipulate, orchestrate and wish ourselves beyond belief. Just get on any *Social Media* platform for 10 minutes, and you'll witness a display of the wonders and accomplishments of people and their perfectly ordered lives.

If we'd all embrace and rest in Psalm 139, verses 13 through 18, we'd be saturated daily with the knowledge of how we were "designed by God."

Consider that God's purposes for each of us are beyond what we could ever imagine. What would happen if we'd just yield to "His plans and purposes" instead of mapping out our life's agenda by ourself without consulting with Him? God is *not* looking for perfection in our minds and bodies in order to be useful for Him.

As in the design of a watch, the watchmaker knows best how it works and fulfills its purposeful design. A tulip never longs to be a rose. Each flower is content with its color, design, fragrance and bloom since that is what it was designed to be.

> *"For it was You Who created my inward part; You knit me together in my mother's womb. I will praise You because I have been remarkably and wondrously made. Your works are wondrous, and I know this very well. My bones were not hidden from You when I was made in secret, when I was formed in the depths of the earth. Your eyes saw me when I was formless; all my days were written in your book and planned before a single one of them began."* Psalm 139:13-18

God "custom designed" each of us to love Him, know Him, and enjoy Him both now and forever. And most of all, we are to "glorify Him" (or in my own words.... **make God look good**) as we live out His plans for our lives.

I've been nourished and mentored by a few amazing women in my life journey, and many of them spoke, shared and lived in ways that nourished my heart to love and trust the Lord, regardless of what was going on in my life. All of these women would have considered themselves very *ordinary*, but they made an *extraordinary* impact in my sojourn.

In several of my stories, I've shared my "life goal" God gave me years ago. It has provided focus, purpose, passion, and direction:

After People Spend Time with Me, What do They Think of Jesus Christ?

I am still learning that it isn't necessary to win every argument, or prove I'm somebody, or even *share* my earthly accomplishments. It is common to hear the following theme from other Christians:

I want to do BIG things, IMPORTANT things for God and His kingdom.

Thankfully, the Bible does NOT mention that concept at all. As Jesus would have it, we are to be faithful in the *little things*. He takes our everyday, simple obedience and uses it in incredible ways. The stories I've shared are all composites of tiny, insignificant elements.

God yearns to show us what He can do when we place *what little we have* in His hand. Every outreach of care, concern, or even baked goods can be multiplied when given to Him to bless others. But we have to start somewhere, and give Him something to work with ... something for Him to multiply.

In contrast to what *we think is important*, God asks us to do what *He knows is important*. It is no accident that most often His ways seem so *"insignificant to us."* Why? I feel it's because we're cannot look through the lens of the Omnipotent, Omniscient Creator, Who *takes the insignificant and ordinary, and makes it of profound value.*

Not long ago, I met a man who shared his passion for loving others into God's family. He spoke of the various *tiny opportunities* God had given him to affirm and love his friend who had sought God through a myriad of religions, only to come to hate all religion.

My friend made it clear that God hates religion too. He wants a *relationship* with us. My friend simply emulated that relationship with his friend. We rejoiced when we heard that recently his friend blurted out:

Looking through the Lens of . . .

"I want to know Jesus, because I know you."

Pause for a moment and re-read his comment. I was blown away with this statement. *He wanted to know Jesus, because of the time spent with his friend. He came to love the idea and the character and life of Jesus, by watching his friend's life.* There's no higher affirmation to receive.

We all live in different neighborhoods, and mix with a vast assortment of people. We're to be "lights in this world" that point to the Savior.

After people spend time with you or me, would they have a clear understanding of Jesus? Could they see an example of serving and sacrifice in action ... just like Jesus who came to earth to die for each one of us – facilitating our forgiveness and restoration of relationship with God.

Like the ORDINARY woman at the well, Jesus spoke to her on an ORDINARY day, in a way that made her life EXTRAORDINARY for her Savior. Her checkered immoral life was transformed right there, and she ran to her town telling everyone about Jesus and the difference He made in her life.

Let's be prayerfully sensitive to every *tiny opportunity* the Lord brings along our path in life to share the love and message of Jesus Christ. For everything *we do or say* should represent how Jesus would reach out to show others His love.

Matthew 10:42 "And if anyone gives even a cup of cold water to one of these little ones who is my disciple, truly I tell you, that person will certainly not lose their reward."

This verse "shouts" that even a *"cup of* ORDINARY COLD WATER," that is tasteless, colorless, and odorless, God will bless and use to reach others; for He notices, uses, and will bless every little thing we do on His behalf, to touch another.

Do People Want to Know Jesus ... Because They Know You?

A CLOSING COMPASS THOUGHT

How do you and I "express God" to others?

Printed in the USA
CPSIA information can be obtained
at www.ICGtesting.com
BVHW030625250823
668843BV00004B/10